ENDORSEMENTS

Tell It Well is an inspirational guide for every aspiring and actual story-teller. **-Frank Viola, best-selling author of *From Eternity to Here* and *God's Favorite Place on Earth*; frankviola.org**

I have known Luke for years and can affirm that his God-given talent to captivate a subject that is so often neglected is second to none. We need to hear more stories of how God's faithfulness has completely transformed lives, and *Tell It Well* contains a few of them. I truly believe this book was written for "such a time as this" and will cause faith to rise in the lives of believers worldwide. To all who read this book, I pray that the Holy Spirit will give you ideas and creativity to tell your story well—it just might change the world!
-Jeri Hill, wife of the late evangelist Steve Hill; president of Together in the Harvest Ministries

Great stories have the ability to connect with and even change the hearts of those who hear them. A well-told story can circumnavigate the globe in a matter of minutes and reach millions, and each one of us have a unique story to tell. Luke Gajary is a gifted speaker and storyteller. I have admired his ability to connect with many different types of audiences and have witnessed crowds hanging on his every word. I have also seen the lasting impact of his words years later. There are bookshelves lined with scores of how-to books on the subject of communication, but *Tell It Well* is not one of them. Rather, it is a call to connect with the heart of your own, personal story and to communicate it clearly. Your story is worth being told, and it is worth telling well to reach a multitude. **-Daniel K. Norris, pastor, evangelist, and author of *Trail of Fire***

Having known Luke personally for eight years, I can tell you this book captures the essence of his life and walk with the Lord. I have witnessed Luke "tell it well" to all sorts of crowds—from small groups in local coffee shops to large gymnasiums full of students. Luke's passion and gifting has always been telling great stories to point people to Jesus. This book lays out a clear and concise message that we all need to grab ahold of.

-Kyle Embry, director of Youth Alive North Texas; author of *Hidden in Plain Sight: America's Unreached Mission Field*

My career has taken me on some incredible journeys—from playing football in the NFL and CFL, bobsledding with the U.S. Olympic team in Russia, speaking to a wide variety of audiences, and owning several successful business. Through all of my experiences, nothing has taken me further in life or opened more doors than the ability to tell good stories and capture the hearts of an audience. Clearly, Luke understands the importance of this concept as well. In *Tell It Well*, Luke uses engaging language and subtle humor to craft a compelling call to embrace and share the stories in your heart.

-Johnny Quinn, U.S. olympian, former NFL player, motivational speaker, and entrepreneur

Stories have been told since the dawn of time; a well-told story can inspire, encourage, and convict others, which is why being a good storyteller is of the utmost importance. In *Tell It Well*, Luke helps the reader find the courage to share their own story by sharing glimpses of his own. He combats our tendency to feel like our stories are meaningless and reminds us that the things we tend to think are insignificant may be more significant than we think.

-Adrian Hummel, Life.Church Online Marketing Leader

Your story is one of the most powerful tools you have to influence those that God brings across your path. As a business owner, I have had the opportunity to share portions of my story with many of my team members, which often leads them to want to know more about Christ. In this book, Luke shares his story and equips others to discover their own stories so they can point to the larger story that God is writing all around us.

-Zach Thomas, Chick-fil-A franchisee in Rockmart, Georgia; author of *Leader Farming: Growing Leaders to Grow Your Business*

I was hooked from the time I received the original first draft of this book—three years before its release. Luke's writing style is engaging, straightforward, and laced with just the right amount of unorthodox humor. Just when you think you know where the story is headed, he throws out another curveball with the precision of a master storyteller. Luke doesn't just offer theology; he invites you into his story and equips you to discover the story that God has put inside of you. I highly recommend *Tell It Well* to all seeking a fresh encounter with God. **-Jared Stump, executive director of Life Impact; author of *Creation & Redemption: Finding Your Place in a Fallen World* and *Identity in Christ***

In a society where good storytelling is undervalued and difficult to come by, Luke reminds us that each of our stories matter and, more importantly, are worth sharing. Testifying to what we have seen and heard God do has the potential to be the turning point in the lives of others, which can spur them to begin their own relationship with Him. **-Allison Abey, campus staff minister with Athletes InterVarsity Christian Fellowship at The College of New Jersey**

Tell It Well reminds us that "The Greatest Story Ever Told" includes our own story—and it's not just a story worth telling but a story that we are called to tell in order to inject hope into a hopeless world. It reminds us to look for the extraordinary ways that God is working within our "ordinary" lives on a daily basis.
-Corinne Karl, young adults director at Park Church in Tinton Falls, New Jersey; former chapter president of InterVarsity Christian Fellowship, Susquehanna University

When I first heard of Luke's book I could not wait to receive my copy, and I am even more excited after reading this important book! Now more than ever, our postmodern culture prefers modern stories over ancient truths. This troubled me until I realized that we as Christians have redemptive stories that carry transformative truths if they are told well. This book will not only inspire you but provide practical

tools to communicate in common language. *Tell It Well* is creative, informative, and very enjoyable—as though you are sitting down for a conversation with the author himself. A must-read for all!
-**Will Ford III, director of Marketplace Leadership at Christ for the Nations Institute; author of** *History Makers* **and** *Created for Influence*

There have been so many times in my life that I have allowed fear of what other people may think stop me from sharing my story. *Tell It Well* not only helped eliminate that fear, it has empowered me and given me confidence to share the things that have changed my life forever. We all have a story, and Luke helps shift our mindsets and guides us to share our stories in a way that can make an impact on everyone we encounter. I absolutely love this book and cannot wait to recommend it to others. Your story matters! -**Ashley Shepherd, author and founder of Beautifully Designed Ministries**

In the heart of every believer is the treasure of their personal history with God. In *Tell It Well*, Luke passionately invites you to see the power in your story by sharing his own story, while inviting the reader to communicate their story with clarity and effectiveness. Once you see the value of your journey with God you connect with the greatest tool to bless others—your life is your message! -**Mark DeJesus, founder of Transformed You and Turning Hearts Ministries; author of** *God Loves Me and I Love Myself!* **and** *Exposing the Rejection Mindset*

Jesus communicated in stories because He knew how impactful they are. *Tell It Well* will help you harness the power of story in your everyday life, in order to maximize the Kingdom impact you make on the lives of others. It is entertaining and you will feel empowered after reading it! -**Ben Debayle, managing director of The Surge Project**

TELL it WELL

FUEL YOUR FAITH & ENCOURAGE OTHERS
WITH THE POWER OF YOUR STORY

Luke Gajary

lukegajary.com

Edited by Jared Stump
Cover and Interior Design by the Nerd Studs (NerdStuds.com)
Author Photography by Cory Hale

Published in Houston, Texas by Battle Ground Creative
First Edition

Battle Ground Creative is a publishing company with an emphasis on helping first-time authors find their voice. Named after an obscure city in Washington State, we currently operate offices in Houston, Texas and Princeton, New Jersey. For a complete title list, please visit battlegroundcreative.com

Special discounts are available on quantity purchases.
For details, email: me@lukegajary.com

ISBN-10: 0-9908738-7-0
ISBN-13: 978-0-9908738-7-7
RELIGION / Christian Life / Spiritual Growth

To Maritza

My story got exponentially better when God wrote you in. I love you.

Contents

FOREWORD

In our short time on this earth, the one thing that will dictate the amount of influence and impact we have will be our story. One of my mentors once told me, "The one who tells the story the most wins the age." Regardless of the arena, the culture, the sphere, or any area of endeavor, the power of the story will prevail. Another one of my mentors—who actually taught me how to tell my story—used to say, "Stories sell; ingredients don't." He was adamant about hammering into people's minds the power of telling your personal story with great passion and conviction.

Our family first met Luke Gajary while he was an intern at a church in the DFW metroplex, which we decided to attend nine years ago. Since that time, I have been able to see Luke grow from a young, vibrant, youth leader to a traveling evangelist, to a husband, to a close, personal assistant, to a father, and now to an emerging author. I've always told Luke that he is a brilliant communicator and has a unique gift to speak to any amount of people in any setting; he is simply a natural when it comes to oral communication. I am quickly discovering he is equally as gifted in his written communication skills.

This book will captivate and inspire you. Most importantly, it has the potential to ignite you to begin the quest of telling your story more often and to more people. You do have a story to tell, and you owe it to yourself to simplify your message, harness its power, and unleash it for the world to hear. You only get one life, and yours will likely have one primary story attached to the end. Paul Revere's life has one story attached, as does Martin Luther King's, Judas Iscariot's, and Adolf Hitler's. Most people, whether notorious or infamous, have one key story attached to their name. I believe that many of you who read this book will come away with a resolve to make sure that your story will be told notoriously when you have passed on from this earth. Luke has a powerful message to share with you that carries the potential to unlock the destiny that you have been called to fulfill. We all have a destiny, and that destiny lies within telling our stories well. The beauty of this book is that it comes from such a fresh perspective, from a young man who has lived the first third of his life very well. He is a young husband and father of two at the time of this publication, and his life exudes character and integrity. He does everything with excellence: at home, in the workplace, or in the church. Luke goes above and beyond to set the standard of excellence wherever he is. The same holds true with this endeavor entitled *Tell It Well*. I love to read books that have something new to offer, something that is organic in its nature. This is what you are about to embark upon in the following pages—a new meal that is organic in its nature and substance. With this being the case, get ready to devour every word, process them correctly, and watch what the outcome will be in your own life. It's time for all of us to "tell it well"—stake claim to your story and win the age.

Danny McDaniel
Entrepreneur
Author of *Power: To Change Your World*
Lead Pastor of Bethel Dallas Church in Lewisville, TX

CHAPTER 1

The Strangest Marketing Strategy of All Time

H e was tired.
He'd been tired before, but this was a whole new level—
"exhausted" would be a better word to describe it. It was different than the type of exhaustion that comes from performing manual labor. Sure, hard work like construction and commercial fishing were exhausting and certainly left one feeling tired at the end of the day, but this was different.

He let out a sigh, feeling some of the heaviness leave as he exhaled. He kicked a few rocks along the path he traveled, if for no other reason than to break the silence—silence that was an unfamiliar, yet welcome friend in these rare moments.

It was early—too early. Yet somehow, it was the perfect time. He had been running hard and fast for weeks. It had all started so quickly and showed no sign of a sustainable, peaceful pace. He was surrounded by people every moment; the crowds had been enthralled since the "wedding incident" and had only grown larger as their curiosity increased. His days were filled with joy and purpose, but he still felt very ... exhausted. The crowds were life-giving, but draining at the same time.

One morning, he woke early and broke away from his colleagues before they were awakened by the harsh rays of the Middle Eastern sun. He was finally alone and able to recalibrate his soul to stay focused on the bigger picture. It was easy to get caught up in the immediate needs of the crowds, the little "fires" that flared up anytime you had to deal with a large group of people. The bigger purpose lingered, however, and in moments of solitude like this one it was soothing to retreat to lonely places and pray.

With each passing moment, he felt his strength being renewed and his passion rekindling. It was as if his soul had taken a dip in a cool spring, refreshing him in every way. He sighed again, but it was a different type of sigh—a sigh of peace and contentment. He could stay here for hours.

The calm was broken by voices. They were off in the distance, but when he heard them, he knew this moment was fleeting like the breaking dawn.

"There he is, guys!" Simon led the group, approaching in a bit of a frenzy.

"We've been looking everywhere for you, Jesus! The people are back—I swear, the crowds get bigger every time! They're eager to hear what you have to say."

Jesus cracked a smile as he stood to his feet, shaking the dust from his tunic as he rose. "Well then, we better get moving! I have a few other towns I'd like to go to. The crowd from yesterday has already heard what I have to say; there are more to teach and heal. That's why we're doing this, right?"

So they began to move. They traveled lean, without too many commitments or roots to tie them down, aside from their unwavering commitment to this wild-eyed man and his revelatory message and miracles.

When they arrived at the next stop, a crowd was already waiting to hear from this mysterious man who they'd been hearing about for weeks. Jesus taught every day in their synagogues and spent a significant amount of time delivering people from their demonic oppression by casting out the darkness.

One day, a leper approached his group of disciples. It wasn't difficult to see him coming, as the crowd parted to allow the man to pass—partly out of disgust that a diseased man would come near them, and partly out of curiosity to see how this fiery preacher would handle this interruption. They'd seem him cast out demons, but this was new.

With a hurried desperation, yet a timid step, the leper neared Jesus. He was used to being dismissed and had grown accustomed to others distancing themselves from him, so he kept a reasonable distance from the man.

He knelt, his voice quivering as he spoke. "If you will, you can make me clean."

There was something about the whole scenario that moved Jesus' heart. The desperation in his approach, the fearful way he spoke, and the open sores that covered his body were almost too much to bear. This was a man that was at the end of himself.

Jesus' eyes welled up. He spoke slowly in an attempt to maintain his composure.

"I will," Jesus said. "Be clean."

Immediately, the man was visibly touched—it was as though his whole body had been dipped in a miracle liquid that renewed his skin and washed his sores away. He gasped audibly when he realized how quickly the transformation had taken place. The crowd began inching closer, trying to get a handle on what they had just seen—or what they thought they had seen. They were still at a fair distance so the details of what had just unfolded were a bit hazy.

The man rose to his feet, astonished and amazed.

In a firm, yet somehow loving way, Jesus quickly grabbed the man's arm in the way a coach grabs an athlete to guide and instruct them. "Listen! You are clean and may go on your way, but this is important—"

The man was captivated.

"Don't tell *anyone* about this. No one! Go, show yourself to the priest, so that he may see what has taken place in your life, but don't share this with anyone else."

The man was slightly confused at the stern nature of this warning, but didn't take it to heart. He knew there was no way he could walk away from this life-changing encounter and *not* talk about it. It seemed Jesus' stern words actually had the opposite of their intended effect— the man couldn't keep what had just happened to himself. One minute he had leprosy; the next minute he didn't. How could one not talk about that?

● ● ●

The scene I've painted above is pretty much straight out of Mark 1, and it baffled me the first time I read it. There's a cross reference to it in Luke 5, and a different, yet similar scenario takes place in Matthew 8. In every occurrence, it's confusing to me, because it goes against everything we've been taught about marketing, networking, and promotion.

Let's frame this story in today's context: Jesus had been a relatively obscure figure growing up, but now, in his early 30's, his ministry was launching in full force. Jesus Christ International Ministries, Inc. (JCIMI) started off with a controversial bang at the wedding at Cana in John 2, and things were rolling smoothly for a startup non-profit. He was gaining a strong partner base, and building a solid core team that carried out JCIMI's day-to-day tasks and logistics. God was speaking, and miracles were happening at his ministry events. It was a powerful time, and the atmosphere amongst the JCIMI team was energetic and contagious. If the past few weeks were any indication of what the future held, they were on the fast track to success.

Then the leprosy incident took place, and Jesus pulled a strange marketing move out of the ministry playbook. In the minds of his team, he should have:

- Set up the JCIMI website, Facebook page, YouTube channel, and Instagram account.

- Put together brief teaching clips set to trendy harp music.
- Assign a couple of the disciples to his social media team, and perhaps hire someone to make a few of those cute quote graphics with hand-lettered fonts.
- Film testimonies (of those like the leper) and blast them out on all social networks.

Obviously these things were not possible in Jesus' day, but I would have imagined this would have been the approach Jesus took, much like modern mega-ministries do with their audiences. Until I read Mark 1.

> *... and [Jesus] said to him, "See that you say nothing to anyone, but go, show yourself to the priest and offer for your cleansing what Moses commanded, for a proof to them." But he went out and began to talk freely about it, and to spread the news, so that Jesus could no longer openly enter a town, but was out in desolate places, and people were coming to him from every quarter.* - Mark 1:44-45

Seriously Jesus? You just changed this guy's life, and you ask him to keep quiet about it?

What was even more strange was how Jesus' request almost had the opposite effect on the man—he immediately told *everyone* what had taken place.

It got to the point that Jesus, from this point on, could not be alone unless he broke away from the crowds and found a desolate place.

Why did Jesus tell the man not to tell anyone that he had been healed? Was it for selfish reasons? Did he not want to be bombarded by crowds and people demanding their own miracles?

I've read some studies that suggest that Jesus wanted the man to first verify with the temple priests that he had gone through a "cleansing" according to the law of Moses (see Leviticus 14:1-32).

But what about the other times? Jesus used this weird marketing strategy repeatedly throughout his ministry.

Here is an example from the Gospel of Matthew:

> *And as Jesus passed on from there, two blind men followed him, crying aloud, "Have mercy on us, Son of David." When he entered the*

house, the blind men came to him, and Jesus said to them, "Do you believe that I am able to do this?" They said to him, "Yes, Lord." Then he touched their eyes, saying, "According to your faith be it done to you." And their eyes were opened. **And Jesus sternly warned them, "See that no one knows about it."** *But they went away and spread his fame through all that district.* -Matthew 9:27-31, emphasis added.

And another example from Mark 5:

While Jesus was still speaking, some people came from the house of Jairus, the synagogue leader. "Your daughter is dead," they said. "Why bother the teacher anymore?"

Overhearing what they said, Jesus told him, "Don't be afraid; just believe."

He did not let anyone follow him except Peter, James and John the brother of James. When they came to the home of the synagogue leader, Jesus saw a commotion, with people crying and wailing loudly. He went in and said to them, "Why all this commotion and wailing? The child is not dead but asleep." But they laughed at him.

After he put them all out, he took the child's father and mother and the disciples who were with him, and went in where the child was. He took her by the hand and said to her, "Talitha koum!" (which means "Little girl, I say to you, get up!"). Immediately the girl stood up and began to walk around (she was twelve years old). At this they were completely astonished. **He gave strict orders not to let anyone know about this,** *and told them to give her something to eat.* -Mark 5:35-43, NIV, emphasis added.

Lest you think these are isolated incidents, here is another example from Mark 7:

Then Jesus left the vicinity of Tyre and went through Sidon, down to the Sea of Galilee and into the region of the Decapolis. There some people brought to him a man who was deaf and could hardly talk, and they begged Jesus to place his hand on him.

After he took him aside, away from the crowd, Jesus put his fingers into the man's ears. Then he spit and touched the man's tongue. He looked up to heaven and with a deep sigh said to him, "Ephphatha!" (which means "Be opened!"). At this, the man's ears were opened, his tongue was loosened and he began to speak plainly.

Jesus commanded them not to tell anyone. *But the more he did so, the more they kept talking about it. People were overwhelmed with amazement. "He has done everything well," they said. "He even makes the deaf hear and the mute speak."* -Mark 7:31-37, NIV, emphasis added.

Does this not baffle you a little bit? Here is the model I would expect Jesus, as the leader of JCIMI, to use:

They sailed to the region of the Gerasenes, which is across the lake from Galilee. When Jesus stepped ashore, he was met by a demon-possessed man from the town. For a long time this man had not worn clothes or lived in a house, but had lived in the tombs. When he saw Jesus, he cried out and fell at his feet, shouting at the top of his voice, "What do you want with me, Jesus, Son of the Most High God? I beg you, don't torture me!" For Jesus had commanded the impure spirit to come out of the man. Many times it had seized him, and though he was chained hand and foot and kept under guard, he had broken his chains and had been driven by the demon into solitary places.

Jesus asked him, "What is your name?"

"Legion," he replied, because many demons had gone into him. And they begged Jesus repeatedly not to order them to go into the Abyss.

A large herd of pigs was feeding there on the hillside. The demons begged Jesus to let them go into the pigs, and he gave them permission.

When the demons came out of the man, they went into the pigs, and the herd rushed down the steep bank into the lake and was drowned.

When those tending the pigs saw what had happened, they ran off and reported this in the town and countryside, and the people went out to see what had happened. When they came to Jesus, they found the man from whom the demons had gone out, sitting at Jesus' feet, dressed and in his right mind; and they were afraid. Those who had seen it told the people how the demon-possessed man had been cured. Then all the people of the region of the Gerasenes asked Jesus to leave them, because they were overcome with fear. So he got into the boat and left.

The man from whom the demons had gone out begged to go with him, but Jesus sent him away, saying, **"Return home and tell how much God has done for you."** *So the man went away and told all over town how much Jesus had done for him.* -Luke 8:26-39, NIV, emphasis added.

Why was *this* not the model of promotion for Jesus' ministry? If I were the head of marketing and PR for JCIMI, I would have instructed everyone who had an encounter with Jesus to tell as many people as possible so the ministry would go viral.

There's a lot of things in the Bible that don't make sense at first glance. This is a big one for me. It may seem counterintuitive to the entire message of this book that you are holding. You may be wondering, "Why even include it?" Or you may be wondering why Jesus would even say this in the first place. Here are a few of my theories:

- He didn't have a solid follow-up and discipleship plan for the influx of new people that would hear the message.
- His Partner Connect database wasn't set up yet.
- He truly did not want the attention. Perhaps for the sake of humility?

Once this book is published, I hope to receive an email from someone with a deeper theological mind who will be able to offer some solid answers.

● ● ●

Penn Jillette, the performer of Penn & Teller fame, was captured on video a few years ago sharing his thoughts on people who don't passionately share their faith. In case you haven't seen it, here's a look at what he said:

> *I've always said that I don't respect people who don't proselytize. I don't respect that at all. If you believe that there's a heaven and a hell, and people could be going to hell or not getting eternal life, and you think that it's not really worth telling them this because it would make it socially awkward—and atheists who think people shouldn't proselytize and who say just leave me along and keep your religion to yourself—how much do you have to hate somebody to not proselytize? How much do you have to hate somebody to believe everlasting life is possible and not tell them that? I mean, if I believed, beyond the shadow of a doubt, that a truck was coming at you, and you didn't believe that truck was bearing down on you, there is a certain point where I would tackle you. And this is more important than that.*

Penn is an atheist, yet he sees the importance of sharing a truth you deeply believe in.

Perhaps Jesus wanted those He touched to be so convinced that they had truly experienced heaven on earth that no persuasion could stop them from sharing their story.

A few weeks ago, I had coffee with a friend who is in the middle of a big transition. He has a great job, but was recently offered two better jobs—at the same time. One is within the organization he currently works for and the other is outside of it. One has a ministry focus, while the other is more entrepreneurial and business-oriented. Both offer unique sets of benefits and challenges.

He told me that his dad is dead-set on talking him out of the ministry position. I asked if it was because it was probably less money.

"No," he told me. "I'm pretty sure he actually does want me to take the ministry position. He's just trying to talk me out of it so that if I do go with it, it will be because I truly feel a conviction in my heart that this is the path God has for me. He wants my motive to be pure, not because someone offered me a certain amount of money or talked me into it."

In the midst of this conversation, my mind wandered to the "never mention this" dilemma I found in Scripture. I wonder if that's why Jesus attempted to silence these people. Perhaps He wanted the story to be pure, to be shared from a place of true passion—not because someone persuaded them to share their story or told them it would be a really good marketing technique.

Since 2009, I've worked for several ministries and businesses in various roles, and my work can be summed up as communications and visual storytelling. I've helped individuals and businesses develop their stories in a visually appealing way that utilizes multiple streams of media.

Over the past eight years, I've noticed a similar thread among many Christians who have had powerful encounters with God.

They are terrible at telling the story.

Whether it is a life changed by the Gospel, a marriage saved from infidelity, a physical healing, financial miracles, or deliverance from drugs, alcohol, pornography, or sex addiction, their life has been transformed, but they have a difficult time articulating what has taken place.

Have you ever cornered a Christian after a church service, in an elevator, or at a coffee shop and asked them to share their most incredible story of what God has done in their life?

Nine times out of ten, it gets weird. They get quiet, their eyes begin to shift, they stare at you awkwardly—it's almost as if they barely know the story themselves.

CHAPTER 2

Why I Wrote This Book

Are you familiar with Julian Smith? In a day and age when people become "YouTube famous," he was one of the original viral stars. In my opinion, he's one of the funniest people on the Internet.

At the time of this writing, he has:

- 1,629,748 subscribers
- 310,072,207 total video views

He's very creative, clean, and hilariously different. *Malk, Hot Kool-Aid,* and *25 Things I Hate About Facebook* are a few of his top hits. You've probably seen some of his content. If you haven't, you have my full permission to put this book down and spend a few minutes watching some of his videos. I recommend those from the 2009-era.

In one video, the character Julian plays has concocted a rather interesting drink, which he offers to a friend. The plot escalates as he keeps getting obnoxiously offended that his friend won't take a drink of the hot Kool-Aid he made using a coffee maker (boy, that was weird to type), and after arguing for some time about why his friend needs to try this amazing drink, Julian finally yells at the top of his lungs, "I MADE THIS...FOR YOU!"

After that video went viral, Julian began using the same quote as a closing logo animation in all of his videos. As the scene would fade to black, his logo would appear, and one would hear an unexpectedly loud, yet familiar yell. It was a touching and strangely personal way to end each piece of content.

If we were in the same room, I would hand you this book and yell the same line, "I MADE THIS...FOR YOU!"

Then people would stare at us, things would get awkward, and you would probably stop following my Snapchat story.

But really, I wrote this book for you. I sort of did it for me, because I had to get what was in my brain and heart out onto paper, but I mostly did it for you, because I wanted to create a resource that would equip people to tell their stories well. I wanted it to be funny, personal, well-written, and empowering, and I feel like I at least nailed three of those. I wanted it to have real stories from my own life, interwoven with helpful nuggets and storytelling principles that could transform the way you see your story.

You know those moments in life that stick with you, those things that someone says—often off the cuff—that you can't get out of your head? I remember hearing a strong, faithful man of God talking about the walk of the believer. He spoke of how, at the end of your life, only one thing will matter: *your personal history with God.*

Did you just attend church, or was your life made up of a series of God-moments that reveal a vibrant relationship with the Lord?

Unfortunately, for many Christians, tangible encounters with God are rare instead of normal.

What if this whole "relationship with God" thing is easier than we've made it out to be?

There's a saying that's been around for years now—on t-shirts, bumper stickers, and even book covers. *Christianity is a relationship, not a religion.*

Do we even know what that means?

I think there are times when this phrase is quoted by people who don't actually have a relationship with God at all. Sure, they believe He is who He says He is, but He's not a part of their day-to-day life.

When I think of this phrase, I picture a couple who has been married for several decades, joyfully recalling their years together as they flip through a photo album. You can always tell when couples have a rich history together; it's almost as if you can feel the love they share.

Remember the time our house flooded and we had to camp out in the backyard for a week?

Remember when we drove that old, junky Civic and we had to turn off the A/C when going up a hill to keep the engine from shutting down?

These are not the moments we spend our single years dreaming about, but they are the moments that make up a rich history of sharing life together—both the highs and the lows. This couple will tell you that holding their relationship together took more than fairy dust or unicorns; it required embracing the gritty side of love that we don't often see posted about on Facebook. It may be challenging at times, but it's a rich and beautiful love that can only come when we embrace both the highs and the lows. This is a deep mystery, how suffering and pain can strengthen a bond, but I've seen it happen time and time again.

Does this sound like your relationship with God? Could the two of you hang out on His front porch drinking lemonade out of frosty mason jars as you thumbed through a photo album filled with memories? Could you sit back and remember the last time He felt so close that you could almost taste His presence? The time you needed a miracle, and He came through at the last minute? The moment you surrendered your life to Him for the first time, and received His life in exchange?

Can you recall the memories? Are they floating on the surface of your heart, or lost somewhere out at sea? More importantly, are you creating new memories? Is your relationship a thing of the present, or just a distant memory from the past?

When you talk about the moments you've had with God, are they forced and robotic, or filled with life? Are your stories filled with dry Christianese, or are they a gushing invitation to jump into an adventure with Jesus? As Christians, the light and hope of the world lives inside of us, but most of us aren't very good at communicating it.

Like all of us, I've had my fair share of ups and downs in my walk with God. There have been times when I felt like I could reach out my hand and He's right there, and other times when He seemed more distant than a cousin you only see every five years or so at a family reunion in Michigan.

During those distant times, it felt like I was grasping at straws. I didn't want to spend time with God because I felt distant from Him, but I was distant from Him because I wouldn't spend time with Him. I had no desire to pray or read my Bible, when in fact that was the very thing I needed to jump-start my relationship with God. A vicious cycle, indeed.

I remember one season in particular, right after I got married, when it felt like I needed a *Back to the Future* moment. I wished I could travel back in time and see the key moments that God had unfolded in my life. I needed to be reminded of our history together—about the love we once shared before I let my heart grow distant. It was strange how forgetful I could be, at twenty-five years old.

I would pick up book after book, longing to be transported back into a meaningful relationship with God. I knew that a book alone couldn't do this, but I still searched. The only problem was, it seemed as though with every book I read the author had already "arrived." There was so much deep theology and knowledge of the Scriptures, but few real-life personal stories—let alone stories of times when they grew distant from God and longed to be close again. After reading countless books—many by renowned authors—there was still a growing need in my soul. Perhaps there was some deep theological truth that I was missing, or maybe I just needed to go back and remember the stories I had already recorded in my personal history with God.

In his book, Chase the Lion, Mark Batterson writes: "Something about going back to a place where God has proven Himself faithful builds our faith even more. It's not just a walk down memory lane. Those memories fuel faith and stoke the imagination."[1]

This is the very reason why I began writing this book. It's the book I wish I could have read during that season in my life. Along the way, I've found that a huge key to this thing called "faith" is the power of story. Deep theology and principles are nice, but it's often the stories of those who have gone before us that give life to our faith. Even the Gospel itself is presented as a story, and each of us have a story of how its truth changed our lives.

In this book, you will find a collection of stories. Some are mine, while some are those of others that have impacted my life. My hope is that these stories will draw you closer to God and give life to your own story, providing the clarity and strength to *tell it well.*

Always be prepared to give an answer to everyone who asks you to give the reason for the hope that you have. But do this with gentleness and respect. - 1 Peter 3:15, NIV

CHAPTER 3

The Power of Story

At the time of this writing, the tallest man who has ever lived is Robert Wadlow of Illinois. Born in 1918, he stood 8' 11" tall, earning him the nickname The Giant of Illinois.

Robert suffered from hypertrophy of the pituitary gland, causing him to produce massive amounts of human growth hormone. This condition led to a continual increase in height throughout his life. By the age of eight, Robert was already 6' 2" and weighed 169 pounds. He was so large that a special desk had to be built for him at his school.

Sadly, doctors were unable to find a treatment for his hormonal imbalance. Robert suffered from various ailments caused by this condition. In 1940, a broken leg brace caused a blister that became infected, leading to his death at just twenty-two years of age. More than 30,000 people attended his funeral, and it took twelve pallbearers to carry his enormous body. Twelve!

Let's travel back farther than 1940, and step into the familiar Bible story of David and Goliath. While Robert Wadlow was the tallest human in modern times, Goliath stood nearly a foot taller!

Judging by the way 1 Samuel 17 describes Goliath, it's no surprise that the Israelites were shaking in their boots at the sight of him.

- Goliath stood at a height of 9' 9"
- His coat weighed around 157 pounds

- The tip of his spear was around 18 pounds

Bottom line, Goliath was a big dude who would have made The Giant of Illinois appear average.

I'm sure you know the highlights of the story. (*VeggieTales* ensured that I was well-informed as a young lad.) But sometimes, we hear stories so many times that we become numb when they are retold—like John 3:16 or the stories your grandpa tells every Thanksgiving. That being said, I want to highlight a piece of the David and Goliath story that you may not be consciously aware of.

While the rest of the Israelites were paralyzed in a state of fear and hopelessness, David convinced Saul that he was the right man for the job of taking on this giant. He possessed an unwavering faith that God had been on his side in the past, making this seemingly impossible task appear possible with the aid of the Almighty Ruler of the Universe.

Let's jump into the story:

And David said, "The Lord who delivered me from the paw of the lion and from the paw of the bear will deliver me from the hand of this Philistine." And Saul said to David, "Go, and the Lord be with you!"

Then Saul clothed David with his armor. He put a helmet of bronze on his head and clothed him with a coat of mail, and David strapped his sword over his armor. And he tried in vain to go, for he had not tested them. Then David said to Saul, "I cannot go with these, for I have not tested them." So David put them off. Then he took his staff in his hand and chose five smooth stones from the brook and put them in his shepherd's pouch. His sling was in his hand, and he approached the Philistine. - 1 Samuel 17:37-40

This is such a wild, underdog story. David rejected the king's armor and moved forward with an unconventional strategy to defeat Goliath.

When you're up against a giant, you can do what everyone else is telling you to do, or you can trust in what you know works—for David, this meant trusting in God and taking the path of faith over the untested armor of the king (which would have appeared to be the far more logical choice to most anyone else). David trusted that God would be with him in this moment, just as God was with him when he defeated the lion and the bear.

Spoiler alert—David wins!

Sorry, I'm that guy. Here's the season finale of the hit show, Jordan Shore (as described in 1 Samuel 17:50-54):

> *So David prevailed over the Philistine with a sling and with a stone, and struck the Philistine and killed him. There was no sword in the hand of David. Then David ran and stood over the Philistine and took his sword and drew it out of its sheath and killed him and cut off his head with it. When the Philistines saw that their champion was dead, they fled. And the men of Israel and Judah rose with a shout and pursued the Philistines as far as Gath and the gates of Ekron, so that the wounded Philistines fell on the way from Shaaraim as far as Gath and Ekron. And the people of Israel came back from chasing the Philistines, and they plundered their camp. And David took the head of the Philistine and brought it to Jerusalem, but he put his armor in his tent. -1 Samuel 17:50-54*

Did you see what I saw?

Something clicked in the Israelites when they saw that David had won. Suddenly, they went from cowering in fear and wondering what this war loss would do to their economy to shouting and storming the enemy camp in triumph. The victory of one shepherd boy turned into a faith-filled victory for an entire army. They saw the giant fall before their eyes, and the triumph that David achieved gave a surge of victory to everyone around him. They were on top of the world. David had unlocked something powerful, imparting a faith into the people of Israel that caused a wave to surge in their hearts as they proclaimed, "God has truly made a way!"

That is the power of story.

And that is the reason why I am passionate about this topic, because I know a good story can change everything; it can rally an entire nation and insert hope into the most hopeless situations.

This is why I become frustrated when believers shy away from sharing the victorious moments when God intervened in their stories and accomplished the impossible.

We've been told that Jesus' death on the cross destroyed the one who has the power of death—the devil (Hebrews 2). Friends, we've already won! The ultimate victory has already been secured; we've got this thing in the bag! Though small wars may wage around us, the larger war has already been won.

So why do the small wars captivate our attention?

Why do they leave us paralyzed in fear?

Why do we forget about the miracles that have already happened?

Why do we keep what God has done in our lives locked inside?

What are the things you have already overcome in your life? They may seem small and insignificant, but your story can breathe life into someone who thinks their story is over. Your story can give hope to someone who is cowering in fear. Your victory can become the victory of another. Your breakthrough can lead to their breakthrough.

But you must share your story. You must talk about your breakthrough. You must share your victories—and even the things you've learned from your failures.

What would have happened if David had sent the rest of the army away so he could defeat Goliath privately? He would have still obtained the victory, but he wouldn't have inspired anyone else to rise up and take action, to pursue and obtain their own victory.

Of course, there are some things that should be kept private. No one needs to hear every detail about your relationship with God, just as I don't share every detail about my relationship with my wife. People don't need to hear about how you pray or read the Bible for three hours a day, but they do need to see snippets of your journey with God—the battles you've fought, the things you've overcome, the victories you've won, and the process by which you obtained these things. People don't just need to see your highlight reel, they need to hear about how you tried on Saul's armor, how you found that it didn't fit, and how you overcame your fear and went up against Goliath anyway—with no armor and inadequate resources to take him down. They need to hear about how God took your weakness, but willingness, to move forward and added His power to give you the victory. They don't need to see your perfection, but how God gave you the victory despite your weakness.

Your moments of frustration and despair that have turned into victory and freedom can give others a much needed surge of faith. Your story can cause the hearts of others to begin to beat with hope again. You never know what might unlock faith in the heart of another.

But none of this will happen unless you tell your story.

Silent victories are great, but they only affect one person. Shared victories have the power to liberate an entire army of people.

When you share your story, it becomes part of a larger story that is much bigger than you, a story that involves the people of God recognizing and stepping into the victory that has already been claimed on the Cross.

Your story is powerful. It's worth telling, and it's worth telling *well*.

CHAPTER 4

Your Story Matters
(I Wish I Was Addicted to Crack)

T he way I was raised has played a significant role in who I am today. My parents instilled the ways of the Lord in me from a young age, and I eventually began to embrace those ways for myself. Not to say that I'm perfect, but my mom and dad made the effort to establish a positive foundation while I was young, and I have built on it as I've grown older.

There's a myth circulating among Christians that says you must have a radical salvation experience in order for your story to really carry weight and make an impact. However, not everyone goes from being incredibly wicked to totally transformed in an instant.

Tim Hawkins, a Christian comedian, has a hilarious bit about how we often view the testimonies of others. He talks about how he was raised in a Christian home, how he attended church, and how he lived a godly lifestyle. Every once in awhile, his church would have a time for folks to share their testimonies.

One day, a new believer took the mic and shared his radical salvation story—the kind of testimony that makes good Christian kids feel a bit insecure about their own. As he began to unravel a mysterious tale of how steeped in darkness he was before he knew the Lord, he told stories of partying, drinking, listening to terrible music, and becoming addicted to crack at the age of seven. In typical fashion, Jesus suddenly got ahold of him and everything changed!

The church erupted in praise as the man stood at the front of the room, beaming with joy at the thought that he was now redeemed. Meanwhile, Tim was sitting on the back row, thinking about how much his own testimony paled in comparison. *I wish I had been addicted to crack. Thanks a lot, God!*

This monologue is often all too true for those who feel like they've been saved their entire life. Instead of rejoicing that they were fortunate enough to grow up in the faith, they begin wishing they had gotten into more trouble so God would have had something to save them from and they would have a better story to tell.

God saving a drunk crack addict on a downtown street corner is not the only type of miracle that causes all of Heaven to rejoice; the angels go crazy when even the most picture-perfect children choose to place their life in God's hands.

Whether we are consciously aware of it or not, even those of us with solid foundations were in need of rescue when Jesus found us. No matter how "good" we may have thought we were, we were still sinners in need of a Savior. Sin is not just sex, drugs, and country music—it's anything that takes God's place in your heart. That's why John warned believers to "keep away from anything that might take God's place in your hearts" (1 John 5:21, NLT).

Sin goes beyond our actions; it includes our inward thoughts and the attitudes of our hearts. That's why Jesus said, "But I say to you that everyone who looks at a woman with lustful intent has already committed adultery with her in his heart ... For out of the heart come evil thoughts, murder, adultery, sexual immorality, theft, false witness, slander" (Matthew 5:28; 15:19).

For those of us who think we are righteous of our own accord, Isaiah warns, "All of us have become like one who is unclean, and all our righteous acts are like filthy rags; we all shrivel up like a leaf, and like the wind our sins sweep us away (Isaiah 64:6, NIV). We may have a solid foundation, but we must still be born again; we must be given a new heart that desires God.

Jeremiah described the condition we are born into quite well: "The heart is deceitful above all things, and desperately sick; who can understand it? (Jeremiah 17:9). Some time later, Ezekiel added to this by prophesying the work of Christ: "I will give you a new heart and put a new spirit in you; I will remove from you your heart of stone and give you a heart of flesh" (Ezekiel 36:26, NIV). Paul described this experience as becoming a "new creation" (2 Corinthians 5:17) and prayed that Christ "would dwell in our hearts through faith" (Ephesians 3:17).

Becoming a new creation in Christ is nothing short of a miracle, no matter how much of a "good Christian" you were. We often discount miracles when they seem—well, ordinary. But our salvation alone is a miracle, and I think it is also a miracle when a couple serves God, provides for their family, and raises their children to love God in a post-Christian society.

Time has shifted my perspective in regard to my testimony. After all, I was not the perfect Christian kid. I had my battles with anger and pornography. But when I think about how much worse things could have been, I feel extremely blessed. Had my parents not built a solid foundation, who knows what road I might have traveled.

There were several key "defining moments" in my teenage years that helped define my relationship with God and set me up for the journey of a lifetime. Some of these moments were seemingly ordinary—connecting with the volunteer youth ministers at my church or attending World Vision events that helped shape my core value of helping those in need. We all have takeaways from our childhood that make us who we are as adults. These moments are both good and bad, and serve as building blocks for the foundation on which we write the stories of our lives.

In his book, *A Million Miles in a Thousand Years*, Donald Miller explores the power of story and the role it plays in our spiritual lives and shares the following thoughts:

> *If I have a hope, it's that God sat over the dark nothing and wrote you and me, specifically, into the story, and put us in with the sunset and the rainstorm as though to say, "Enjoy your place in my story. The beauty of it means you matter, and you can create within it even as I have created you."*

> *I've wondered, though, if one of the reasons we fail to acknowledge the brilliance of life is because we don't want the responsibility inherent in the acknowledgement. We don't want to be characters in a story, because characters have to move and breathe and face conflict with courage. And if life isn't remarkable, then we don't have to do any of that; we can be unwilling victims rather than grateful participants. But I've noticed something. I've never walked out of a movie thinking all movies are meaningless. I only thought the movie I walked out on was meaningless. I wonder, then, if when people say life is meaningless, what they really mean is their lives are meaningless. I wonder if they've chosen to believe their whole existence is unremarkable, and are projecting their dreary life on the rest of us.* [2]

God has created you to live a life that tells a story within the larger context of His Story. But not all of us live as if we have stories to tell. Not all of us are willing to courageously embrace the internal and external conflict that comes with defining and telling your story to the world. Fear has a way of holding us back from living a good story and telling it well; it tricks us into settling for a boring life of chasing the American Dream, where our greatest aspiration becomes owning a Mercedes or a big house in the country. While this is not inherently bad, it doesn't make for a very interesting story if this is all you are living for.

A few years ago, my friend Jared wrote a great book called Creation & Redemption: Finding Your Place in a Fallen World. When he launched the book, he had some t-shirts printed as part as his promotional campaign and book tour. One of the designs was a simple blue shirt with large block letters across the front, which read:

YOUR
STORY
MATTERS.

No matter how much you've been through or how little you've been through, your story matters. Everything happens for a reason and nothing is ever wasted—not your greatest failures, your deepest pain, or even the moments that seem to be insignificant.

We often think we have to go through seasons of deep darkness or reach the highest heights in order to have a story to share with others. But what if the moments that appear ordinary are the moments that make the most impact? You will never know unless you tell it, and before you can tell it, you must believe in the depths of your heart that your story matters.

The righteous flourish like the palm tree and grow like a cedar in Lebanon. They are planted in the house of the Lord; they flourish in the courts of our God. They still bear fruit in old age; they are ever full of sap and green, to declare that the Lord is upright; he is my rock, and there is no unrighteousness in him. -Psalm 92:12-15

CHAPTER 5

A TV and a Broken Toe

My relationship with God began with a TV and a broken toe. I was seven years old, living in Eastern Pennsylvania at the time. My dad is one of the strongest believers I know, so I grew up attending church with my five younger brothers and sisters.

My earliest memories of church took place in a small town called Macungie, which was a forty-minute drive from our home in Easton, PA. I have strong memories of that old church building, mostly the ugly, red carpet and Sunday School classes.

Though my current friends may find this hard to believe, I was a fairly quiet kid who was often nervous and shy. I didn't like Sunday School at first, because of a minor mishap on my first day. We were going around the room doing the introductions, and when the teacher asked me to say my name, I quietly responded, "Luke."

The middle aged man with a friendly smile and thick, dark hair that was showing hints of grey, strained to hear. "Lou?" he questioned.

I froze. *What? No! Didn't he hear that last letter?*

Unsure of what to do, I nodded. Close enough, I guess.

I was the new kid, and for the next several weeks, I was Lou.

While he did eventually add a fourth letter to my name, I can't recall how that happened. My parents must have heard him refer to their oldest son as "Lou" and set the record straight.

Aside from that incident, I loved Sunday School. The regular adult service was boring, but Sunday School was where it was at.

Because flannelgraphs.

What a classic teaching tool! Some things will never be replaced by fancy new iPads or Apple TV's. Whatever happened to those things?

Flannelgraphs taught me the basics. You know, the stories everyone learns as a church kid—the reason why Jesus came to earth and why a relationship with Him is important.

What flannelgraphs didn't teach me, I learned from my dad. He taught me a lot about God from a young age, led us in praying together as a family, and made sure we were in church every Sunday. Often, it seemed like we would learn things that were beyond our maturity level, but looking back, I see that he was simply pouring the concrete for a solid foundation that I would build upon later on in life.

Because I was the oldest of six, I tended to be fairly independent—a trait that has carried over into adulthood. On one day in particular, I was exercising my independence by doing something I thought would be helpful. As I recall, my dad had moved our only TV from downstairs to the upstairs master bedroom. This was long before the days of slimline LED TV's, so ours was one of those large, boxy sets that looked like it had a Volkswagen attached to the back of it. We didn't have cable, and only got three local channels—the only one of interest being PBS.

After moving the TV upstairs, Dad temporarily set it on the bed. He had the intention of moving it to the top of a dresser, but got caught up in something else.

I found myself alone in the room. Determined to be helpful, I decided that I would move the TV from the bed to the dresser by myself.

Vastly underestimating my own strength, I was doomed from the start. From the moment I lifted the TV off the bed, I knew I couldn't handle it. But it was too late; I was already committed. Needless to say, gravity won this battle, and the massive weight of a 1990's-era TV that was almost as big as I was came crashing down on my big toe.

It was the most excruciating pain I had ever felt; the only natural reaction was to scream my head off. My parents came running into the room to see what all the commotion was about.

Everything that happened after that was a blur. While I can't recall the details, I remember my toe was severely bruised and either broken or dislocated. Despite the pain, I don't think we went as far as going to the emergency room.

What I do remember was what happened later that night. Once I realized that I was okay, I settled down and went upstairs to my room. I then began to think, if something as silly as a TV landing on my toe could cause so much pain, what if something worse were to happen?

That is when I began to think about eternity.

At seven years old, I began to ponder. What if something were to happen to me that would take my life? Where would I spend eternity?

I remember kneeling down on the floor of my room and sincerely asking Jesus to come into my heart that night. Knowing that something tragic could happen, I didn't want to end up in hell on a technicality—because I didn't pray a prayer.

Do I believe I was truly saved that day?

To be honest, I'm not sure.

I prayed a prayer, but my life wasn't really any different after that point. Granted, I was only seven, so it wasn't like I was being rescued out of a lifestyle of sex and drugs at that point; I had simply made a conscious decision to allow Jesus into my heart. That is what I had been taught and understood at the time, and it was a decision that I reached on my own, without my parents even being present.

When I recall my salvation experience, this is the story that first comes to mind, as it was the first time I had thought about eternity and responded. This was a starting point for me, but I eventually progressed into a deeper relationship with Jesus. If all I had ever done was pray the salvation prayer I learned from the flannelgraphs, and then moved through life without a living and vibrant connection with God, I'd be much more lost than found.

Still, what happened that day with the TV and my [possibly] broken toe opened a door in my heart as I began to confront the reality of death and the question of eternity, which I had not previously given a single thought. That day, I became aware—though not necessarily consciously—that there was more to this "relationship with God" thing than simply going to church.

I'm reminded of Revelation 3:20: *Behold, I stand at the door and knock. If anyone hears my voice and opens the door, I will come in to him and eat with him, and he with me.*

If you're reading this book, I assume that you have had a similar moment in your journey. After all, the goal of this book is to help believers to better articulate their stories, whether yours was a radical conversion from a place of deep darkness, or a "pseudo" salvation experience where nothing really happened aside from praying a prayer or responding to an altar call.

Can you articulate this part of your story? Can you put to words the moment you first encountered Jesus and began following Him?

When my wife, Maritza, and I go out on the weekends, we love to visit Southlake—a wealthier town about fifteen minutes from our house in Fort Worth. They have a nice, outdoor shopping center that is set up like a giant square. In the middle are fountains, benches, and great restaurants, while shops and more casual restaurants line the edges. A small park is situated at one end, with rows of luxury brownstone townhouses facing it.

As we walk along the streets on that end of the square, we often wonder what it would be like to live in one of these homes. They're rare in Texas, though much more common in the Northeast where I grew up. While we love our small, suburban "starter" home, we can't help but imagine what it might be like to live somewhere else.

One day, a festival was taking place in the square when we visited with our young daughter. As we were walking through the park, the brownstones came into view and my wife and I began talking about them, as usual. As we talked, I got out my phone and began looking at the prices of homes that had recently sold. As we already knew, they were way beyond what we could afford in this stage of life (one cost nearly ten times as much as our house!), but it was fun to just look.

I suppose this is why many people buy lottery tickets—they get a taste of a vision that is bigger than what they are currently living and, for a moment, they are captivated by a glimmer of hope at the thought of what could be, if they only had more money.

As I scrolled through my real estate app, our pace slowed. We gazed across the street, seeing the homes on the screen come to life before our eyes. Suddenly, one of the front doors opened. A man in his mid-50's came out, a beer in each hand.

It was 11:00 a.m.

Upon noticing us staring at his house, he smiled and waved as he walked down the front steps and turned down the sidewalk toward the festival. Suddenly, he stopped, turned around, and motioned for us to come across the street. He was remarkably friendly for a stranger, so we threw caution to the wind and began to cross the street.

"You guys wanna buy a townhouse?!" he blurted out as we were about halfway across the street.

I don't know if it was his personality, the alcohol, or a little of both, but he was very chatty.

I politely laughed, motioning to the stroller that held our 18-month-old. "Sorry, sir, we've already got a nice place nearby where this one has a yard to play in. But we love this area and were just wondering what it's like to live here."

"Man, I f***ing love living here! It's great!"

He went on to tell us how he lived there with his girlfriend, how close they were to the nightlife, and how well the area fit his lifestyle—which apparently consisted of a lot of drinking and Ubering.

"You sure you don't want to buy a townhouse?" he asked again. "Ours is about to go on the market in a couple months; we're moving out of state!"

Once again, I politely laughed. "Sorry, sir, but we're good."

"Well, do you at least want to see the inside? I saw you admiring them from across the street; wouldn't you like to check out the inside?"

I was up for it, but hesitated when I noticed the nervous look in my wife's eyes.

"Come on," the man beckoned. "Why the f*** not?"

Because I don't even know your name, you're nearly inebriated, and this is how horror movie trailers always start.

This is what I imagined was running through Maritza's head. I shot her a look that said, *Come on, it'll only take a minute—and it'll be fun!*

She nodded apprehensively, which was my cue to lug the stroller up the front steps and into this stranger's house. Once inside, we were given a tour of the entire downstairs and small backyard. The man acted as though he was the realtor, providing us with details like the square footage, pricing, and even some juicy information about the neighbors. We complimented the home and chatted with the man about his family before parting ways. We left reminded that there are still strangers that are friendly and welcoming.

The most interesting part of this whole encounter was how readily this guy let us in his home. (I still don't even know his name!) He didn't know us, we weren't interested in buying his house, and it wasn't the 1950's anymore.

Many of us enter a relationship with Jesus in a way that is similar to how the man let us in his house. We see Him observing from across the street and wonder what He's looking at, what He wants from us. We politely approach Him and, perhaps, invite Him in to look around the first floor of our lives. However, there is no real commitment, no access given to the more intimate parts of our lives, not even an exchanging of names. We know He won't be staying long, so there's no need to change what we've got going on or give a thought to what it might look like to have Him living here with us; we're just inviting Him in to make us feel good and give us the opportunity to show off what we've built or acquired. It's casual, nonchalant—or, as the man from the townhouse would say, "Why the F not?"

Does this sound like your salvation experience?

Are you truly committed to following Jesus, or are you simply entertaining a guest in your home? Have you surrendered control of your life and made Jesus not just your *Savior*, but your *Lord*?

Take a moment to do some soul-searching. Examine your personal history with God. Ponder the words of this Scripture from Revelation 3. Set this book aside if you need to.

The story that is in you, the story that is waiting to be released to the world, begins when you encounter Jesus and your life is forever changed.

> *I know your works: you are neither cold nor hot. Would that you were either cold or hot! So, because you are lukewarm, and neither hot nor cold, I will spit you out of my mouth. For you say, I am rich, I have prospered, and I need nothing, not realizing that you are wretched, pitiable, poor, blind, and naked. I counsel you to buy from me gold refined by fire, so that you may be rich, and white garments so that you may clothe yourself and the shame of your nakedness may not be seen, and salve to anoint your eyes, so that you may see. Those whom I love, I reprove and discipline, so be zealous and repent.* **Behold, I stand at the door and knock. If anyone hears my voice and opens the door, I will come in to him and eat with him, and he with me.** *The one who conquers, I will grant him to sit with me on my throne, as I also conquered and sat down with my Father on his throne. He who has an ear, let him hear what the Spirit says to the churches.* -Revelation 3:15-22, emphasis added.

CHAPTER 6

Where It Really Began

I would love to take all of the credit for my relationship with God. It would be cool to say that one day I simply had a revelation of my need to know Him and embarked on a soul-searching journey. False.

There have been many that have gone before me, so many men and women that laid the foundation for the faith that was passed on to my parents, who in turn passed it on to me. Legacy doesn't happen by accident; it's more often something that is imparted to us rather than something we create on our own. The ceilings of our parents and grandparents become our floors as we push forward into the future, reaping the harvest from the seeds they sowed years and even decades before.

My dad was actually the first person in his family to come to know Jesus, something I find to be quite remarkable. He literally added a new root to his family tree and began a new legacy. I'm so grateful that he made the decisions that he did, as they are the reason why I'm part of this Story today. My story is not my own; it began with my dad, and I'd like for him to tell his story in his own words.

This is Ted Gajary, and I'm excited to get to write a little in my son's first book. I'm so proud of him and my five other children as well.

I grew up in a small town in New Jersey. My parents weren't Christians and didn't attend church, but they often sent us to the Methodist church next door. As I grew older, I lost interest and stopped going.

When I was in the seventh grade, my best friend, Ralph, moved away. I didn't really have any other friends in the neighborhood, but became friends with a boy down the street named Eddie. His family went to a different church, and they began taking me with them to Long Hill Chapel in Chatham, NJ every Sunday and Wednesday. This went on for many years.

This church taught that we needed to give control of our lives to God. Over a period of time, I came to agree with what was taught and considered myself to be a Christian, but I never responded to any of the calls to repent and give my life to God. I did, however, make many friends. Some were believers, while some were not.

When I was seventeen, one of these friends gave his life to God, and I saw some major changes take place in his life. It was then that I realized that this stuff was real, and that I needed to get serious about it. I needed to make a decision, so one night, during a children's Christmas service at church, I surrendered my life to God.

From that point on, my life changed dramatically. I had previously struggled with depression and suicidal thoughts, but that quickly came to an end. I would later discover that some of my friends' parents had been aggressively praying for me—thank God for that!

It was my senior year of high school, and I changed my college plans in order to attend a Christian school in New York. Around this time, my parents went through a divorce. My mom became a Christian during this season, and felt God calling her to become a doctor, so she went back to college and on to medical school. She became a doctor and worked in Alaska and Oklahoma until she retired. My dad remarried and eventually became a Christian as well.

I was excited about my new life as a Christian, but I was also frustrated that I still messed up and fell into sin on a regular basis. I asked people about this, and was encouraged to pray more and read the Bible. I was already doing that, so their feedback wasn't all that helpful.

As I read the Bible more and more, I learned about the concept of *walking in the Spirit.*

> *For freedom Christ has set us free; stand firm therefore, and do not submit again to a yoke of slavery. But I say, walk by the Spirit, and you will not gratify the desires of the flesh.* -Galatians 5:1, 16

The more I read about walking in the Spirit, the more I became focused on learning how to do it. I discovered old books like *Abide in Christ* by Andrew Murray and *The Normal Christian Life* by Watchman Nee. These books, and others, taught me what it meant to *abide in Christ* (John 15:1-17), *take off the old self* (Ephesians 4:22-24), and *count myself dead to sin* (Romans 6:1-14).

Being dead to sin was something that I honestly didn't understand. *What does that mean? How does it change the way I live?*

I read more books, and even attended a few seminars. Eventually, it began to click, and the real breakthrough came when I read what Jesus taught about *counting the cost* in Luke 14.

> *Now great crowds accompanied him, and he turned and said to them, "If anyone comes to me and does not hate his own father and mother and wife and children and brothers and sisters, yes, and even his own life, he cannot be my disciple. Whoever does not bear his own cross and come after me cannot be my disciple. For which of you, desiring to build a tower, does not first sit down and count the cost, whether he has enough to complete it? Otherwise, when he has laid a foundation and is not able to finish, all who see it begin to mock him, saying, 'This man began to build and was not able to finish.' ... So therefore, any one of you who does not renounce all that he has cannot be my disciple."* — Luke 14:25-30, 33

That was when I realized I hadn't truly counted the cost; I hadn't made up my mind in advance to follow Jesus in every situation. Instead,

I was trying to figure out what to do in the midst of each temptation. From that moment on, I resolved that I would follow Jesus, no matter what. This changed everything. Now I wasn't trying to figure out whether or not I would follow Jesus when I was tempted; my sole focus was on doing what He was calling me to do. I finally felt like I was making progress in my walk with God. It was like finding a path in the middle of the jungle. I wasn't out of the woods yet, but the going sure was a lot easier.

It's kind of like when you are fasting. You've made a commitment ahead of time to sacrifice. Normally, you eat any dessert that comes your way. But when you're fasting, you simply don't eat those things—because you're fasting. You made up your mind ahead of time, not when you were presented with a plate of cookies.

After I made up my mind that I would follow Jesus—no matter what—I went through a sustained time of walking in the Spirit. I'm talking about walking in obedience and submission, day in and day out.

While in college, I began dating a girl who had experienced what she called "the Baptism in the Holy Spirit." One night, she asked if she could pray for me to experience this as well.

"Sure, knock yourself out," I replied.

Some time later, when we were praying together, it happened. I felt like I had put my finger in an electrical socket. In that moment, I also felt God speak to me and tell me that I could sing. This excited me, because I enjoyed singing worship songs, but never could quite seem to get the notes right.

After this experience, I began to receive some very dramatic answers to prayer. Many of these occurred during the weekly street evangelism trips to New York City that I was involved in. We were praying daily, and each week, I would meet people who were open and ready to respond to the Gospel. A marked difference was seen in the number of people who were getting saved during our Friday night outreaches.

On one occasion, I was approached by a guy who asked me if I could help him.

"Sorry," I replied. "I don't have any money for you."

"That's not what I mean," he said. "My life is a wreck and I want to talk to you about Jesus."

Week after week, we saw remarkable things like this take place!

I had been preparing for full-time ministry at Nyack College, but one day, I realized I was full of pride. As I prayed, I felt God tell me that I needed to be a sheep before I could be a shepherd.

After graduating from Nyack, I moved into the City to serve at a church I had previously worked with. I found a job as a teacher, but the salary was low, so I got a second job at a Christian bookstore. While working at the bookstore, I met a guy who invited me to attend a different church in my neighborhood. He wouldn't take "no" for an answer, so I eventually attended an event at that church. It was there that I met another teacher whom I quickly befriended. He and I later became roommates, and he would introduce me to my new circle of friends, which included a young woman named Shari.

Shari's sister had led her to Jesus, and she had followed His leading to take a teaching job in the City. I was in love, but didn't want to marry anyone who wasn't willing to go wherever God might lead. So I took Shari to the worst area I could possibly think of—the South Bronx. I asked her if she would be willing to move there if God called her to, and she said "yes." She said "yes" a second time when I asked her to marry me shortly thereafter.

A friend of ours had planted a church in the Bronx for Cambodian refugees. They threw us a traditional Cambodian wedding feast, which was wonderful. I was amazed that these folks had strong, happy, and healthy families—even though they didn't have much money or even speak English.

After Shari and I were married, we left the City for New Jersey, and eventually ended up crossing the Delaware to Easton, Pennsylvania.

The Cambodian refugees had taught me to trust God to provide for my future family, so we didn't wait until we could "afford" kids before having our first, Luke.

During this time, the small group we were a part of went through an inner healing program, which culminated in a trip to Pittsburgh for a conference. There I experienced a breakthrough moment related to something that had happened in my childhood, which caused a stoical disconnect between myself and my emotions. My newfound freedom took a little getting used to, as I was now feeling things I had never felt before. Where I had previously been emotionless in certain areas of my life, I now could not speak publicly without getting choked up.

Eventually, we had a total of six kids, and I had a good job with a small, but growing company. We homeschooled the kids, and our little house in Easton was growing crowded. A door opened for a new job with a company in Texas, and we decided to walk through it. We moved to a bigger house near Fort Worth, where we've been ever since.

There's an ever deeper legacy here that goes back further than my dad, but that is a conversation for another book.

As this chapter comes to a close, I ask you: Do you know what your legacy will be? And do you recognize that your story is being built on top of a story that is already in motion?

CHAPTER 7

Healing: A Powerful Encounter

D uring my pre-teen years, my family left the church with the flannelgraphs and began attending another church that was just a few blocks from our house and seemed like a natural fit. My best friend, whom I had known since kindergarten, went there. The church was fairly small, but it felt like home; it felt like family. The pastor and his wife were a very sweet, older couple—you know, the kind of people who would be the perfect grandparents in a Hallmark movie. Their smiles would light up a room, which was easy to do since the room wasn't very big. We let our roots grow down into the soil. My dad got involved in leadership and my siblings and I quickly made friends in the youth group.

This church was a Mennonite church. Typically, when I tell someone I was raised in a Mennonite church, they give me a funny look as if to say, "Go on ..."

I think most people have a picture in their minds that Mennonites are a few light bulbs and a TV away from being Amish. I wasn't aware of this stigma until I left Pennsylvania and moved to the Bible Belt, where the church landscape seems to be composed entirely of Southern Baptists and Pentecostals.

Growing up, this was simply "my church." I didn't understand all of the denominational differences, so I didn't think much of it. But the more I go back and learn about the Mennonites, the more intrigued I become. I wish I had been aware of the rich history of this movement when I was right in the middle of it, but sometimes you have to step back from something to fully appreciate all that it is.

For a short, but detailed history of the Mennonites, I invite you to turn with me to the Global Anabaptist Mennonite Encyclopedia.[3] And yes, I can say that three times fast.

In 1906, the Pacific Coast Conference of the Mennonite Church (MC) resolved that all ministers, evangelists, and members having the baptism of the Holy Ghost should encourage all other believers to seek the experience of the baptism of the Holy Ghost.

In 1954-55, Pastor Gerald Derstine and a number of young people from Strawberry Lake Mennonite Church in Ogema, Minnesota began to experience unusual signs of the Spirit, such as speaking in tongues and being slain in the Spirit. Conference officials asked Derstine to clarify publicly that at least some of these activities were of the devil, but he refused to do so. Therefore, in 1956 the conference withdrew his ministerial credentials, thus prompting him to leave the denomination. They later apologized and welcomed him back to the Mennonite Church in 1977. Other members experienced the baptism with the Spirit throughout the 1950's and 60's, often without revealing it publicly.

In 1970, retired missionary Nelson Litwiller experienced the baptism with the Spirit in a Catholic charismatic prayer meeting in South Bend, Indiana. He provided significant leadership to the charismatic movement in the Mennonite Church until his death in 1987. "Festivals of the Spirit" were held at Goshen College in 1972 and 1973, which were attended by several thousand people. Some lay leaders and ministers planned a church-wide charismatic conference in 1974, held at the Landisville (Pennsylvania) campgrounds and a second one at the Missionary Church campgrounds (Goshen) in 1975.

The official response of the MC came in several ways. In 1972, a consultation was held on the person and work of the Spirit at Eastern

*Mennonite Seminary in Harrisonburg, Virginia. In 1974, the General
Board appointed a task force to develop a statement on "The Holy
Spirit in the life of the Church" to be brought before the General
Assembly in 1975. The assembly called for certain congregations to
study and improve the statement. With some changes, it was adopted
in 1977 as a resource for teaching throughout the denomination,
giving a favorable response to the charismatic movement.*

*In October of 1975, a few dozen individuals met at Youngstown,
Ohio and formed Mennonite Renewal Services (MRS). The purposes
were to provide consultative and liaison services to individuals and
conferences, to represent charismatic Mennonites to groups within
and beyond the denomination, to converse with leaders of the
Mennonite Church, to provide information and referral services,
and to sponsor teaching ministries and conferences. Nelson Litwiller
represented MRS on the planning for the Conference on Christian
Renewal (interdenominational charismatic conference) at Kansas
City in 1977 and for the North American Congress on the Spirit
and World Evangelization, held in New Orleans in 1987. Mennonite
Renewal Services has reported to each Mennonite Church (MC)
General Assembly and has been affirmed in its work by Mennonite
Church General Board. The leaders of MRS sought to renew the
church and to encourage renewed members to stay with the church
and not to leave it.*

*A significant factor in the renewal in the Mennonite Church (MC)
has been renewal conferences. Mennonite Renewal Services continued
holding church-wide conferences until 1978. Annual regional
conferences emerged in 10 to 12 areas across North America. The
MRS organization also held annual consultations involving persons
active in renewal ministries throughout the church. People from other
Anabaptist and Mennonite groups were invited to participate in the
early stages of this development. While some members of other groups
joined MRS, no official delegates were sent more than a few times.*

*In April of 1987, MRS decided to change its name to Believers Church
Renewal Ministries and incorporated people from the Church of the
Brethren renewal ministries. This was the result of working with*

these leaders for several years. By 1989, the new body was known as Empowered Ministries. This organization continued until 1995 when reduced financial support prevented its continuation.

In a 1986 survey that polled one-third of MC congregations, pastors reported 10 to 15 percent of the members called themselves charismatic. Between 25 to 30 percent of the pastors themselves identified as charismatic.

● ● ●

I remember there would be times when the Spirit would move in our Mennonite church, but I was never quite sure what to make of it. Looking back, I wish I had dove headfirst into this move of the Spirit, instead of allowing my lack of understanding and fear of the unknown to keep me on the edge of wonder.

I've noticed that we Christians tend to avoid things we can't wrap our minds around. We do this a lot with God—when we don't understand what He's doing, we hold a part of ourselves back, we settle for safe, and we often end up missing out on His work. God does not invite us to come to Him and get all of our questions answered; He simply invites us to say "yes" to a lifelong journey of wonder as we discover more and more of who He is. We come to Him with questions—and we may actually leave with more questions—as we struggle to wrap our minds around the mystery of a God who is outside of time and space, but is yet present with us through the power of the Spirit.

Like any teenager trying to figure out life, I had my questions and doubts. Until one day, when God blew them to smithereens.

My first real, tangible encounter with the Holy Spirit happened when I was fourteen.

We lived in an extremely old house in Easton, built sometime during the 1890's. It required a lot of maintenance, and my dad tried to stay ahead of the needed repairs since he hoped to sell it and move our growing family into a larger house. Nearly every weekend, we would be expected to help paint, refinish hardwood floors, replace plaster with sheetrock, pour concrete steps, and patch cracks in the sidewalk. Some days, it was all hands on deck, and we would be paid hourly for our work.

One day, I was working on fixing some cracks in an exterior wall. As I lifted bags of concrete mix, I threw out my lower back. Like most guys, I rarely spoke up about such injuries. Despite the excruciating pain, I kept quiet.

The pain came and went for several months, and I accepted that this was my new normal. I could still function, but experienced quite a bit of discomfort most days.

During this time, our church held a series of special revival services. To be honest, I was more interested in hanging out with my friends at the time, so I didn't pay much attention during these types of events. The Holy Spirit was still a mystery to me, and I thought He was reserved for the uber-spiritual, such as the three old ladies who always sat on the front row and were especially lively during worship.

After a week of nightly revival services, the Sunday morning gathering was a unique one. The residue of the revival meetings lingered in the air, and at the end of his sermon the pastor gave an altar call for those who desired a special touch from God. I didn't fully understand what this entailed, but was so fed up with my back pain that I was willing to give God a chance.

Back then, my biggest concern was what my friends thought, so going forward required me to swallow my pride. As I approached the altar, the pastor greeted me with a smile and asked what I needed prayer for. I motioned to my lower back and explained that I had been experiencing pain on and off for a few months.

He sat me down in one of the chairs on the first row, then knelt in front of me. Looking me in the eye, he spoke in a pastoral voice like that of a grandfather.

"Luke, do you believe God can heal you?"

I still wasn't sure how I felt about all of this. I had seen new and intriguing things happen all week. My heart was being stirred, but I wasn't sure how to respond—or if I even wanted to respond at all.

Despite my reservations, I felt my head nodding.

Placing his hands on my calves, he gently took ahold of my legs.

"Okay, then. We're going to ask God to heal your back."

He went on to whisper a quiet, yet deeply profound prayer. From the moment he opened his mouth, I began to feel an intense heat in my lower back, which quickly spread down into my legs. With my pastor cradling my calves, my legs began to lift out of his hands—entirely on their own. I didn't move them, and he wasn't lifting them—in fact, he wasn't even touching them. Yet, they somehow began to rise into the air. The heat intensified, but I didn't feel any pain; it was peaceful and calming. I then felt a gentle "pop" in my lower back, and the feeling of heat in my lower back began to slowly fade.

My pastor was grinning from ear to ear, probably because the look of awe on my face was a dead giveaway that something had happened. It honestly wasn't the most dramatic thing in the world. Sometimes, I think we expect the miraculous to be this over-the-top, noisy thing. But in my case, it was somewhat ordinary—aside from the heat in my back and my legs lifting up on their own. What was undeniable was that I had been touched by God. There was a joy that came from knowing that God saw my pain and healed it, even though I was a doubting, arrogant teenager.

I was healed! From that moment on, I never again dealt with chronic lower back pain. I still didn't fully understand what had happened from a theological perspective, but I walked straighter, stood taller, and resolved that there was power in the name of Jesus—to break every chain, and to heal my back. I didn't fully commit my life to God on the spot, I didn't get called to ministry, I didn't go out and get business cards that read "Luke Gajary: Healing Evangelist"—in fact, I rarely told people about my experience. Although I was convinced that God's power was real, I still had to work through some things.

I don't know where you stand on the issue of divine healing from a theological perspective. Perhaps you are a firm believer that God still heals today, or perhaps you have your doubts, as I did. Wherever you're at, that's okay—for real.

I could throw out a list of Scriptures, break down the theology of healing, and go into a mad frenzy of apologetics, but instead, I'll leave you with this:

And when Jesus entered Peter's house, he saw his mother-in-law lying sick with a fever. He touched her hand, and the fever left her, and she rose and began to serve him. That evening they brought to him many who were oppressed by demons, and he cast out the spirits with a word and healed all who were sick. This was to fulfill what was spoken by the prophet Isaiah: "He took our illnesses and bore our diseases."
-Matthew 8:14-17

Here's the takeaway: If Jesus will heal a mother-in-law, He will heal anyone!

Just kidding (kind of).

He took our illnesses and bore our diseases.

What are some illnesses and diseases you're experiencing in your life? Do you realize that Jesus has already taken and bore them in Himself?

I realize those reading this come from a variety of backgrounds. You may come from a church background that didn't believe healing is "for today," or personal experience may have closed you off to this aspect of God's character. Regardless of your background or experience, I want to ask you the same question my pastor did on that day when this fourteen-year-old kid got radically healed out of the blue. Do you believe God can heal you?

Perhaps you're on the other side of the coin and you have seen God move miraculously, bringing healing to your life. Do you articulate your story well to others?

CHAPTER 8

Purity: A Better Way

I As I progressed in my faith journey, I developed stronger and deeper relationships with other kids in the youth group at my church. Since I was homeschooled, this was my primary social experience. We were at the age where everyone was beginning to become interested in relationships with the opposite sex, and I certainly had my eyes on a couple of the cute girls in the group. Yet, as I watched my peers begin the pointless journey of dating in middle school, I felt in my gut that there had to be a better way. Something just didn't feel right about introducing romance into the lives of fifteen-year-olds—who can't legally operate a car without a parent in the front seat.

It was then that Steve and Mary, my youth group leaders, had us begin a group study for teens, which we watched on VHS. Yes, you heard that correctly—VHS.

Back then, Joshua Harris was a young, up-and-coming author who had written a popular book entitled *I Kissed Dating Goodbye*. It was still fairly new, but was becoming widely popular in Christian circles across the nation. Some of the leaders at my church heard of it and thought it would be beneficial for the youth group to do the VHS study.

As I sat in the youth room of a small Mennonite church in Pennsylvania, watching a VHS tape on an old TV set, I thought to myself, *This is what I want for my life.*

This immediately became a pivotal moment in my story. I had felt there was a problem for some time, but wasn't sure how to handle it. My friends were going in one direction and there seemed to be no other alternative, but this study presented a better way. This may not be your experience but, at the time, it was what I knew was right for me. I had seen the wasted emotions and unnecessary wounds being inflicted on the hearts and minds of my middle school peers, and I did not want to go down that road. By the grace of God, I was presented with an alternative while I was still at the crossroads. I chose that path, and it has made all the difference in my life.

Isn't it interesting how seemingly insignificant choices can make a huge impact? Take Steve and Mary, for instance. I drove them crazy at times, and they may not have thought they were making much of a difference when they would hang out with us on Wednesday nights. However, years later, myself and at least dozen others have been deeply impacted by their love and countless volunteer hours.

At the time of this writing, *I Kissed Dating Goodbye* has sold nearly one million copies worldwide. It hasn't been without controversy, however, as some regard it as being a legalistic solution to a problem that has been blown out of proportion.

What I find most remarkable about the book is that Joshua Harris wrote it when he was just 21 years old. It was published a few years later, and offers an inspirational call to a life of sincere love, purity, and purposeful singleness. Love it or hate it, this book has turned the Christian singles scene upside down. Years later, the conversation continues, as young people explore biblical alternatives to our cultural norms.

● ● ●

Promise me, O women of Jerusalem, not to awaken love until the
time is right.
-Song of Solomon 8:4, NLT

Solomon penned these strong and compelling words about romance outside of the correct timing. He speaks of a better way, the path I found by learning from Josh's mistakes. As my youth group went through the VHS study, I resolved in my heart not to awaken love until the time was right.

Though I made this counter-cultural decision as a teenager, please don't think this meant I was automatically perfect. The truth is, I struggled with pornography for several years. However, I resolved not to waste time and emotions on dating before I was ready, and by the grace of God, I was able to follow through with this commitment—with a little help from my parents and mentors. I didn't pursue any deep, romantic relationships until I knew I was ready to get married. Not that I shunned women entirely; I did have friends of the opposite sex, but I was pre-determined that these would be friendships and nothing more—until I was ready to pursue the one woman I would marry. Upon making this decision at fifteen, I wasn't sure when my time to date would arrive, but I knew it was in the distant future.

When I was twenty-one, I met Maritza. She was the first girl I ever truly dated, and I married her at age twenty-four.

She was my first kiss.

The woman I gave my virginity to.

The first and only woman I've ever loved.

I could write an entire book on how we met and how I knew she was the one, but to be honest, it's a story that I prefer to keep between us and our closest friends.

I will tell you this—God's way is better.

It doesn't mean you have to embrace this exact concept. I realize that you may be older than I was when I made this decision. You may not be in a place to make the choice that the first person you date will be the person you marry.

There's grace if you've messed up along the way. God makes all things new, and when you make the decision to save yourself for the love of your life, God makes all things possible. It will take hard work and focus on your end, but I can tell you that it's worth it.

Take heart—there's a better way that this world has never known.

> *The world takes us to a silver screen on which flickering images of passion and romance play, and as we watch, the world says, "This is love." God takes us to the foot of a tree on which a naked and bloodied man hangs and says, "This is love."*
>
> -Joshua Harris

I have learned that this part of my story is quite valuable when I speak to young people. For a period of time, I worked with an organization called Youth Alive. We would do middle and high school assemblies, which was a secular environment. Instead of one person monologuing students for half an hour, the director developed a speaking team that would each take segments of no more than ten minutes. The school administrators would ask us to speak about a variety of topics, which usually revolved around bullying, the negative effects of sexual promiscuity, and developing a "winning" mindset.

I would do the sexual promiscuity segment, and talk about how abstinence had made a difference in my life. Perhaps what made this talk so impactful was the fact that I had actually lived it.

When I would take the stage to share my story, I would begin by saying, "My name is Luke! I'm twenty-two years old, and I am ... a VIRGIN!"

Sometimes I would yell the last part.

Then I would wait.

The first time I did this, I was afraid that the students would laugh at me. In that moment of silence, I would have flashbacks to my teenage years. I wasn't the cool kid, all over again.

In reality, one of two things would happen. There would either be dead silence, followed by a few chuckles from the guys, or a brief pause, followed by thunderous applause (which was mostly from the girls in the audience).

Believe it or not, the second scenario happened more often than the first; I received more applause than awkward silences and laughter. On several occasions, I would be approached afterward by students—both male and female—who were inspired and grateful that I had shared my story, as it gave them the inspiration and courage to walk down this road themselves. For many who had internally made this decision, but were being sucked in by the culture of their school, hearing my story gave them the guts to go against the grain. It may be hard for some to believe, but there are more young people who place a value on abstinence than we might think.

There will be pieces of your story, glimpses from your journey, that you will be afraid to share based on your perception of how you will be received. Chances are, these perceptions are not reality, sharing your story will have a greater impact than you think, and people will be inspired by the things that you hold in low esteem.

There is thunderous applause for you and life change for others waiting on the other side of sharing your story. Will you move past your fears and rise to the occasion?

CHAPTER 9

Satisfied, Yet Hungry For More

66 Okay kids, I really want you to listen to this."

My dad had gathered us in one of the bedrooms of our small home in Pennsylvania, an audio cassette in his hands.

"God has done a powerful work in this man's life," he said as he loaded the cassette into the stereo. "I want you to hear about his salvation experience. It's pretty intense."

The testimony of a former drug addict turned preacher began to play. I remember the level of passion in his voice. He had been in a place of deep despair and God rescued him.

This man was Steve Hill. My dad followed his ministry from a distance, and would occasionally receive materials and messages on cassette in the mail.

Steve began drinking at the age of ten. By sixteen, he was using cocaine, heroin, and morphine. He was heavily dependent on drugs and alcohol, which caused him to commit multiple crimes that eventually led to a felony conviction. One Saturday morning when he was just twenty-one, his body began to shut down due to his heavy drug abuse. For three days, he experienced extreme convulsions and was in a lot of pain. But then, on October 28, 1975, Steve's mom invited Hugh Mozingo, a Lutheran minister, to see him.

"I can't help you," the minister told the young man, "But I know someone who can and His name is Jesus."

In a moment of desperation, Steve began to say the name "Jesus" and the convulsions immediately stopped. He gave his life to Christ on that day and never looked back. On the cassette recording, Steve said he was immediately set free from his addictions to drugs and alcohol when he surrendered to Jesus. He became a minister, and was part of a large-scale revival in the 1990's, which took place at Brownsville Assembly of God in Pensacola, Florida.

In 1993, Pastor John Kilpatrick changed the order of the Sunday night gatherings at Brownsville from a typical service, where the congregation heard from guest speakers, to a time of prayer for revival in the nation and in the Church. Steve Hill visited one of these early meetings, which were before the revival officially started. He would later share a journal entry from one of these nights, which read, *"If the Lord is going to pour out His Spirit anywhere, it will be at Brownsville."* [4]

In this entry, Steve continued to testify of seeing children prostrate before the Lord, some of them with fingernails sinking into the carpet, weeping and interceding over the condition of their unsaved loved ones. It was "deep calling unto deep" in his own heart, and in the hearts of those in the congregation. A spontaneous and abnormal moving of God's people to prayer has preceded remarkable seasons of Holy Spirit outpouring at multiple points in history.

As the great evangelist Jonathan Edwards once said, "When God is about to do a mighty new thing, He always sets His people praying."

These prayer meetings went on for a few years. Then, on Father's Day (June 18, 1995), God stepped down. On this particular Sunday morning, Steve Hill visited Brownsville to preach. This 41-year-old evangelist had already preached all across the country, not to mention Europe, Russia, and Argentina. He carried an insatiable burden for lost souls, which often drove him to tears as he preached messages of repentance and forgiveness.

The service was only supposed to last a few hours, but continued until 4:00 in the afternoon. The evening service, which was scheduled to begin at 6:00 p.m., lasted until 2:00 on Monday morning. "Then the same thing happened the next night, and the next night," Pastor Steve told the Toledo Blade in 2001.

"John Kilpatrick looked at me and said, 'If it goes a day, it'll go six weeks,'" Pastor Steve told the Blade. "And six weeks is a long revival. I said, 'Whoa, I can't imagine that!'"

The revival did indeed continue for six weeks—but it didn't stop there. Pastor Steve had been scheduled to leave for Russia on June 19, but he ended up canceling that trip and clearing his calendar for the next several months, which turned into years. As the Blade's religion editor put it, "The Rev. Steve Hill was asked to preach for two hours on a Sunday morning in Pensacola, Fla., and ended up staying five years."

Word quickly spread about what God was doing at a seemingly random church in the Florida panhandle, tucked away from the high-traffic tourist centers on the state's coastline. The inner-city church had a 2,200-seat sanctuary, and people would begin lining up in the morning to ensure their seat for an evening service. These services would often go until well after midnight, and people would stand in the Florida humidity for *hours* just to get in!

To accommodate the sudden influx of visitors, the church built a second 2,200-seat sanctuary across the street and showed the services live via closed-circuit television. In all, between 2.5 and 4.5 million people attended the revival from 1995-2000—with crowds reaching as high as 5,500 on a single night for several nights in a row. These people came from all across the country, as well as 128 foreign countries, and represented a variety of denominational backgrounds. More than 200,000 people gave their lives to the Lord, over 200 people were sent out as overseas missionaries, and countless more were refreshed and renewed with a newfound passion for God that compelled them to live set-apart lives marked by holiness, worship, prayer, and evangelism.

Professor Vinson Synan, a leading Pentecostal historian and dean of the Regent University School of Divinity, has called it "the largest local church revival in the history of America." In addition, he wrote that "Brownsville, with its emphasis on conversion and people weeping over conviction of sin, seems to be a revival in the long tradition of American native revivals dating back to the preaching of Jonathan Edwards. There's heavy preaching on sin, repentance, conversion, and holiness. And there's a lot more weeping and wailing over sin than there are the so-called exotic manifestations."

While the revival formally came to an end in 2000, the move of God that had begun in the hearts of His people carried on. Steve Hill relocated to Dallas and planted Heartland World Ministries Church a few years later in 2003.

Coincidentally, after years of searching for a home that would better accommodate our large family, my dad received a job transfer to Texas in 2005. We settled in the suburbs of Fort Worth and immediately began attending Heartland Church in Irving, which was about forty-five minutes away.

The timing of our move was perfect. I was about to enter my senior year of high school, and we were getting plugged into a new church over the summer. On one of my first Sundays to visit Heartland, a random kid my age walked up to me and introduced himself. His name was Travis. I was new, a bit shy, and not sure what to expect. I guess it showed.

Travis walked me around the building, asked me questions, and introduced me to his circle of friends, as well as the youth pastor. All on my first Sunday! This warm welcome immediately made me feel at home. All of my doubts about this new church, new state, and whether or not I would actually make friends were significantly diminished in just a few hours.

Heartland was a game-changer for my friendships, but also for my faith. This church was serious about God; to them, church wasn't a game or social club. My interactions with Travis and his willingness to go the extra mile to connect with the dorky, new kid began to tear down the religious walls around my heart as I became open to the work that God wanted to do in my life. My entire experience at Heartland was a landmark that would forever alter the trajectory of my life.

Isn't it remarkable how a single smile and handshake can change someone'e life? We tend to downplay these simple church experiences, focusing so much on the production aspect of Sunday morning that we miss the relational components that can be pivotal in the lives of first-time guests. We become so focused on how the music sounds, what type of backdrop is on the stage, the condition of the parking lot, and the layout of the bulletin—all good things—that we forget about the more important things. None of these elements profoundly impacted my life; it was a random church member going out of his way to connect with me that broke down my walls and erased my doubts and fears.

One author wrote about a church visit that he dubbed The Cold Congregation.[5] He was visiting a church that appeared to be quite welcoming. The parking attendants greeted him with beaming smiles, eagerly pointing in the right direction so he knew exactly which door to enter. The greeters at that door shared their enthusiasm, offering warm smiles and firm handshakes as they held the doors and handed out bulletins.

"As I made my way through the foyer into the worship center, I knew I had found the perfect church," he writes. "But as soon as I made it past all the professionally loving volunteers, I was confronted with ice. There was no more welcoming, warm feeling. The folks in the room gave me looks like, 'Who is this guy? Why is he in our church?'. It appears the leadership at the church desperately wanted guests, but the congregation missed the memo."

Ouch.

I am thankful that this wasn't the case at Heartland. In fact, Travis and I remain good friends to this day.

The same day that Travis reached out to me, the youth pastor mentioned to my parents that he would be taking the students to a youth conference in a few weeks. Though it was short notice, he said he would make room for me if I wanted to go. We talked about it later, and I decided to give it a shot. I thought it would be a great opportunity to connect further with other students and perhaps make a few new friends. Little did I know what God had in store for me there.

A few weeks later, myself and a few dozen other students loaded into the church bus and made our way from Dallas to Pensacola for the Branded by Fire conference at Brownsville Assembly. It was July of 2005. Up to this point, I had not made up my mind where I stood in relation to God. Though I was raised in a Christian home, I had never been positioned or pressured to take ownership of my faith and decide whether or not I wanted to follow Jesus for myself. I was comfortable, and thought the "broken toe prayer" and attending church twice a week was enough—until this trip to Pensacola. I had also had Charismatic experiences in small doses, but there were questions lingering about Pentecostalism and what made it unique compared to other Christian traditions.

For the first two days of the conference, I took the position of an observer and held back. I recall one of the messages that was preached was a throwback to the crucifixion, a very dramatic, illustrated sermon that peaked with the question Pilate asked in Matthew 27: *What shall I do then with Jesus which is called Christ?* (verse 22).

In that moment, I knew I had to answer that question as well.

What did I really believe?

And what was I going to do with Jesus?

Would I continue to ride on my childhood prayers and the faith of my parents, or would I dive into discovering who Jesus was for myself and make my own decision to follow Him?

These questions made their way in and out of my mind, but I continued to observe.

Then day three came. I was away from my everyday context, away from my parents—I hardly knew anyone at the conference—and away from the pressure to choose the same path as someone else. Something happened that night. I'm not sure what it was, to be honest; I just know that during the worship service, something changed in my heart.

I had separated myself from the group and could feel a weighty presence begin to descend upon me. To this day, I can still hear the chords of the worship song that was playing that night in my mind. I suddenly began to weep—yet strangely, I was completely at peace. I lifted my hands in an act of surrender as the tears streamed down my face. What I felt was unexplainable, yet undeniable. No one prayed for me, no one laid their hands on my head—there wasn't even an altar call! God and I were simply having a moment.

In that moment, I told God I didn't want to live by my own strength any longer. I wanted to follow Him, and I surrendered my life into His hands. I wanted to fully embrace His work in my life—even if that meant some "strange" stuff that I didn't fully understand. I was willing to learn and to follow. The future prospect of the American dream suddenly seemed dim and lifeless compared to the joy of following God's call. Something shifted that day, as I have felt a newfound freedom in worship and increased love for God ever since.

The following summer, I returned to Florida once again for the Branded by Fire conference. This time, I received the Baptism in the Holy Spirit, which brought a new power and strength to my life and walk with God.

For all who are reading this, whether you have been on this journey with God for a few days or a lifetime—or perhaps are still exploring what this whole faith thing is all about—I want to pray for you. I pray that your hidden passions, your deep desires, your quiet longings, the things that keep you up at night as you stare at the ceiling; I pray that these things would be awakened in your heart in a new way, that you would discover the life you were created to live and refuse to settle for anything less.

● ● ●

My wife could eat the same things, at the same restaurants, over and over. She loves Chick-fil-A, Olive Garden, and a few others places. She could order her meal without looking at the menu, and be perfectly content to enjoy what she already loves without trying anything new.

I'm the exact opposite. I've got to try the new place that just opened up or the little hole in the wall that no one really knows about, except the locals. If we go to a place we've been to before, I want the Chef's special of the day. Take me somewhere where they are serving sea urchin; I want to try something I've never tried before.

A few years ago, I was at a ministry conference in downtown Dallas. Maritza and I weren't married yet, so I was on my own. The conference ended at 4:00pm on Saturday, so after I mingled a bit, it was nearly dinner time. Since I was on my own, I decided to do something a bit different than I would have if Maritza was with me. I had a good book in hand, and wanted to sit down and get some interesting food. Like any good Millennial would, I hopped on Yelp and found this little Italian place. It was close by and had abnormally good reviews from what I would expect to find in the area.

I was a bit skeptical when I pulled up. This place was a hole in the wall, the kind of place where you wonder, "Are they even open, or did they close their doors ten years ago?"

As I entered the small, dark dining room, which had enough of a crowd to let me know it was a good spot but not so much of a crowd that I was overwhelmed, I knew I was in the right place. As I was guided to my seat, I attempted to make out what the host was saying to me. She had a very thick accent, which I recognized to be Italian! While those of you back in the Northeast would expect an Italian family to run an Italian restaurant, this is not the norm in Texas.

"This is going to be some good food," I thought to myself as I took my seat.

I decided to order something the Yelpers spoke very highly of—a pasta dish with spinach and pork.

After ordering, I held back from eating too much of the bread that was placed on my table. I didn't want to miss out on what was to come.

When the highly-anticipated dish arrived at my table, it looked and smelled amazing—and it tasted absolutely incredible, just as I had expected. It was a magical experience for my taste buds, and I was craving a few more bites as my plate grew empty. It left me wanting more.

I previously worked in the restaurant business for seven years, and one thing I learned was this: If you desire to give the customer an above average experience, you don't want them to leave full and satisfied.

Isn't this interesting?

As an owner or chef, you want to leave your customers wanting more—you want them to be craving "just one more bite" as they clean their plate.

Why is this?

So they will come back!

If they recall leaving your restaurant wanting more, they'll come back for a second round.

However, if they leave full and satisfied, the experience can easily slide into the "average" category. They didn't leave upset, but there wasn't really anything that "wowed" them, either. I left the Italian restaurant in Dallas wanting more, and as a result I've thought about going back ever since.

This was the same experience I had with God in Pensacola during the summer of 2005. Though I have been connected with God since this day and have become satisfied in Him, there's a growing hunger for more. I was no longer content to just go to church twice a week; I had to have God in my life on a day-to-day basis.

I pray that you would have the same attitude and experience in your own relationship with God, that you would experience Him, and that He would satisfy your soul—but at the same time you would be left craving more. A.W. Tozer said it like this, "To have found God and still to pursue Him is the soul's paradox of love, scorned indeed by the too-easily-satisfied religionist, but justified in happy experience by the children of the burning heart."

We serve a God who can be found, but still be sought after. He makes Himself known to us, yet there is always more of Him to discover. King Solomon said it like this, "It is the glory of God to conceal things, but the glory of kings is to search things out" (Proverbs 25:2).

Sometimes, God hides things from us so we can "search them out." He's not hiding *Himself* from us; rather, He doesn't give us the answers to all of life's questions right away. Instead, He extends an invitation to journey with Him and grow deeper in love as we discover who He is. In doing this, we step into our destiny as kings and priests of God (Revelation 1:6).

May your heart always burn to discover more of who God is as you discover who He has made you to be.

CHAPTER 10

Crazy Kyle and the Gap Year

T he summers of 2005 and 2006 forever changed my faith. I was now "Spirit-filled" or "charismatic" or whatever term you might use to describe my experience. For me, it wasn't so much about a label as it was the reality that I went from being a nominal Christian to feeling a deep hunger to pursue God and involve Him in every area of my life. I had tasted and seen His goodness (Psalm 34:8), and I was hungry for more.

I felt a call to ministry, and wanted to live for something larger than myself. The typical American Dream of three kids, a house with a white picket fence, two cars in the garage, a dog, hamster, and an all-around comfortable life in suburbia was suddenly of little appeal.

Instead, I wanted to live a life of complete surrender to the will of God. While I now realize this is just as possible for a family living in the suburbs as a missionary in Africa, at the time, I was willing to do whatever it took to know Christ and make Him known.

I credit much of this spiritual appetite to the leaders who mentored me at the time, one of whom was the late Steve Hill, the Brownsville evangelist and pastor of Heartland. It was in this church that I was connected to a great youth ministry where my heart was set on fire for the Lord. Pastor Steve had a fire in his eyes and a passion in his belly that was unmatched. In my opinion, a minister with deeper conviction, a stronger call to holiness, and more fiery altar calls remains to be found. He passed away in March of 2014, and the hole that was left in the Body of Christ is still felt.

When I graduated from Central High School in the quintessential suburban community of Keller (a suburb of Fort Worth), I knew that I didn't just want to go to a big university and pursue a bachelor's degree—even if it was a Christian college and the degree had a ministerial focus. Not that there's anything wrong with college; I just knew it wasn't what God had for me. My dad didn't understand this decision at first, perhaps because he grew up in the Northeast where most middle-class families expect their kids to go to college (which isn't as high of an expectation in the South).

Over the past ten years, there have been many churches and organizations across the country that have started one to two-year ministry schools to provide a "training ground" for those called to ministry. These ministry schools provide a theological framework, but focus heavily on the practical side of ministry and actually preparing a young minister to "do the stuff" that they feel God is calling them to do.

Pastor Steve had recently established a ministry school to accompany the new church plant, bringing men and women from all walks of life (and numerous locations across the country) to Irving, Texas to attend Heartland School of Ministry (HSM).

When I graduated from high school, HSM was a happening place. I had friends who attended the school, and loved that Pastor Steve taught a few of the classes himself and personally interacted with the students. It would be a true honor to train under this man, and I felt this was the direction that God was leading me in.

My dad was initially hesitant with this decision, but agreed to let me take a gap year and try it out. The program was two years, with an optional third year internship after, but my dad wisely recommended I start with the first year, and then we could discuss the possibility of my returning to complete the second year.

Essentially, a "gap year" is an intentional season after high school where you focus on discovering who you are as a person—what you're passionate about, what motivates you, what makes you feel empowered, among other things. Instead of making the leap from high school to college in two months, you take a year off and focus more on developing yourself as an individual than developing your skill set. Some use this time to take part in an internship, some work, some travel the world and/or spend a significant amount of time abroad, and some do something else entirely. It's a time to meet new people, try new things, visit new places, and have new experiences.

This may sound a bit flaky to some older folks, perhaps merely a "millennial thing." However, it has been proven to be successful by renowned universities, including Harvard, Princeton, and Yale—not to mention Time Magazine and Education.com. All report that students who spend their first year after high school experiencing some aspect of "real life" are eventually more productive in their adult careers and family endeavors, compared to those who transition directly from high school to college, giving them eight years of student life that is often void of connection to the "real world."

This concept is still catching on in the United States, but is widely accepted in Europe. In Western Christian circles, a gap year usually refers to participation in a non-accredited internship program or "school of ministry" established by a large church or para-church ministry, such as YWAM. Some students take part in these internships for a year and go on to college, others take a gap year and go directly into the workforce, and there are even some who decide to commit several years—or their entire lives—to these organizations.

These internship programs encourage students to seek God's best for their lives—whatever that may be. Sometimes it may align with where they thought their life was headed, while other times it may be something completely different. It's really cool to see God intervene in someone's five-year plan and take them from student to teacher in the very program that they participated in during their gap year. This may not be the path for everyone, as God may call some to go back to college after their gap year, which they have the flexibility to do—not to mention the confidence that comes from knowing they are on the right track, because they didn't just jump from one thing into another.

I loved attending HSM and learned a ton there. It helped shape my character and define the course of my life, especially because everyone was there for the same purpose and the hand of God was on each of our lives in one way or another. There were only a few dozen of us in each graduating class, which made relationships with the opposite sex a bit interesting. This was further complicated by the fact that everyone was making an effort to focus on the Lord, and we wanted to be sure that we didn't detract from the work He was doing in our lives. It was clear that typical, college dating scenarios would not work in this group.

A few of the guys responded to this by creating a "pick-up line" system. It was mostly a joke, but this technique in which to spark romance between two students would often go something like this: "Hey girl ... what's your calling? Missions work?! No way; mine too!"

I say this was mostly a joke—but then serious relationships started popping up all over the place. They might as well have changed the name from "School of Ministry" to "School of Matrimony" (and off the record, a few of us did!).

I was enrolled in the youth ministry track of HSM, which I found to be very fulfilling. This gave me a chance to be creative and connect with students—and have a lot of fun doing it! Not only was my heart for the next generation further established, I was given the opportunity to gain hands-on experience on top of solid, doctrinal teaching. My heart was being enlarged along with my head, meaning everything I learned in the classroom was instantly applicable in the "real world," rather than just being stored up there somewhere, turning me into an ego-maniac like many college students these days.

Much of what I've learned has stuck with me to this day. As I was writing this book—several years later—I flipped back through my journals from the HSM days and ran across this quote from Pastor Steve, which I wrote down during one of our chapel services.

The first thing I look for in any young man or woman when it comes to the ministry is PASSION. Just passion. Because the preaching skills will come. You don't have to be a great orator or have an incredibly lengthy education, or even have degrees on the wall if you have passion.[6]

Even though my heart was on fire for the Lord, I still had a foggy view of what the future held. Initially, I was going to attend HSM for one year and then transition to pursue a bachelor's degree from a state university—a move I thought would make my parents happy. Even though the school of ministry was a two-year program, I fully immersed myself during my gap year. I fulfilled all of the school's requirements, served in the local church (which was conveniently located in the same building), dove deep into the Scriptures during my classes, and maintained a part-time job on the side to provide some spending money.

I see so many eighteen to twenty-year-olds these days who are very confused about their lives. They get so caught up in their next steps—what college to attend, what field to study, where they will live after they graduate—that they'll wind up switching majors several times and even change colleges on a whim. This not only wastes time, it racks up a lot of unnecessary debt.

I am all for attending college—but sometimes it takes more than a few months to really make a solid decision, and most students don't even get that much time. As the pressures of high school are winding down, they spend their senior year looking at colleges, and have often made a decision before they graduate. The problem is, this decision is often made in the hustle and bustle of high school life (even though senior year is slower for many students). Once they graduate and the pomp and circumstance fades away, they're often hit with the reality of their decisions that seemed great at the time. *What did I just get myself into? Do I really want to attend college in another state? Is nursing even the field I really want to be in for the rest of my life?!*

I use this example, because there are some majors that you don't just "get out of" once you're in them. You can't just take your nursing degree and go be an engineer—or vice versa. This leads many students to choose generic majors such as "business" and wander aimlessly for a few years—and, sadly, sometimes for all four years. They then graduate with a ton of debt. Rather than launching into a promising career like their parents, they end up back at home, still unsure of what they really want to do with their lives.

This problem has been amplified with my generation and those that follow. A lot of people want to rag on us for being too flaky, but in reality, there is often this unspoken pressure that is way more intense than what was put on previous generations. Social media further complicates this, as we're constantly bombarded with the "perfect" life our friends are living, and feel our own lives don't measure up.

While it's not the end-all, I think an intentional gap year is often the solution to these newfound problems that paralyze emerging generations. The key word here is "intentional"—it's not just sitting around and playing video games for a year, but taking some of the pressure off and putting oneself in an environment that fosters growth in all areas of life—personally, professionally, and in relation to God.

For me, I found this at a school of ministry, but God may have a different path for you (or your student!). My relationship with God was solidified during my gap year, and I'm not sure where I would have ended up if I would've gone straight from high school to some big, party school.

I'm not saying that your gap year should always lead to ministry - in fact, I am on the journey of a lifetime but it doesn't look like how I originally envisioned it. The end goal of "taking some time to figure things out" is not to enter traditional "full time ministry". That's how things happened here, but as time progressed and through following God's leading, I later entered the workforce(as you'll read about later in this book). I have since discovered that my calling is a dual-purpose one, a unique handcrafted artisanal blend of business and ministry.

I've seen the pressure for young people go both ways.

1. Follow the path of your parents, pursue tradition four year education, get a degree, and spend decades in the workforce living a comfortable life.

2. Ignore tradition, it doesn't work: just do what you're passionate about and the money will come.

I've seen people succeed in each method, and I've seen people fall flat on their face, waking up one day wondering what they did wrong.

I'm not trying to get you to either embrace the pressure or ignore the pressure for your future. I simply encourage you to take some time and really figure out what it is that you're passionate about and where that fits. Could be traditional college, could be a ministry internship, could be traveling with a group of monks in Indonesia. Plus, you may find later that God hits "reset" on your career - for example, my grandmother graduated medical school and became a doctor at 50 years old! You have a long time to figure your life out, and a life surrendered fully to God can be truly taken anywhere.

At the end of my first year, my dad saw the fruit in my life from my time at HSM and his mindset about my future began to change. He saw that I didn't fit in the traditional, four-year college "box," and gave me his full blessing to stay at Heartland, because He saw what God was doing in my life there. I ended up completing my second year, graduating, and then spending a third year doing an internship at the church. The goal of this internship was to submerge students in the inner-workings of the church, so they could pursue outside ministry opportunities at the end of the third year with a wealth of both knowledge and hands-on experience under their belts. During this time, I learned that I enjoyed being around people more than I enjoyed being in a church office. Don't get me wrong, it takes a lot of effort and behind-the-scenes work to make the visible ministry happen, but I had an itch to rub elbows with the people!

My church internship was in the youth department, and one of my roles was to visit high school students who attended the church at their school lunches. This not only enabled me to interact with students, it got me out of the office. I also helped out with a variety of tasks during our weekly youth services at the church. I saw God do a lot of cool stuff, both inside and outside of the church.

At the close of one of our services, a student approached me. I recognized him, as I had met him while visiting another student's school and invited him to our youth services. He was one of those kids that was a bit ... rough around the edges. We'll call him Kevin.

The service was quite evangelistic, and the preacher that evening made a strong appeal for students to draw a line in the sand and get rid of anything holding them back in their relationships with God. He then gave an altar call, and dozens of students flocked to the front. However, instead of going to the front, Kevin came and found me in the back of the room.

"Hey, Luke, you know how that guy was, uh, talking about giving up things that hold you back?"

I fist pumped in my head.

"Yeah ..." I said aloud.

"Well, let's say—hypothetically—that someone had something on them—physically, literally—that they needed to get rid of. What should they do?"

"Well, Kevin," I replied, trying not to crack a smile. "Hypothetically, I'd tell this person to head out back to the dumpster and physically, literally get rid of it. Then, hypothetically, they could pray and get their heart right as well."

"Can you show me where the dumpster is?"

Kevin followed me out back, behind the church, where I watched him dispose of several clear baggies that were stuffed with something I couldn't identify, but later found out was marijuana—about $150 worth. Before the service that night, his plan was to smoke some of it and sell the rest. Instead, he disposed of his stash, got his heart right with God, and got plugged into the church.

Week after week, we watched story after story like this unfold. Nothing compares to watching God work in people's lives in real, tangible ways. This ruined me for cute Bible studies and "ministry as usual."

● ● ●

I loved working with the youth ministry, and the idea of becoming a youth pastor seemed promising, but I wasn't completely sure if this was the right life path for me.

We were in class one day when the instructor, Daniel (who was also the youth pastor at Heartland and my mentor), brought in a U.S. missionary who worked locally, in North Texas. His name was Kyle, and he was the director of Youth Alive, a ministry that partners with local churches across the region to bring the Gospel to public schools by empowering students to reach students.

He talked about how our schools are an unreached mission field that is hidden in plain sight, right in our own American backyard.

I was immediately hooked by his message. He spoke with such purpose and clarity, and I felt like I was hearing words that resided deep in my own soul; they just hadn't made there way to the surface yet.

Finally, I've found something I can see myself playing a role in! My heart was burning with joy as I thought of how I might be able to become involved with this ministry.

After Kyle finished speaking, I approached Daniel and told him, "Everything that Kyle shared with us ... sounds like the stuff I have pictured myself being involved in. I think I've found the type of ministry I want to work with."

"Go tell him that," Daniel replied. "He's just getting started in this new role, and I'm sure he'd love to discuss how you might be able to be involved."

A few weeks later, Kyle and I had lunch together—and we met for many more lunches in the weeks that followed.

We discussed Kyle's vision, the vision of Youth Alive, and what the future of this organization would look like in North Texas. Since I would complete my internship at Heartland in two months, we also discussed if there might be a place for me on the Youth Alive team. And it just so happened that there was.

I took the position of missionary associate and spent the next two years traveling with and learning from Kyle. Something about our personalities and callings clicked. We had similar senses of humor and heartbeats for evangelism. I had finally met someone who was "doing the stuff" I could see myself doing—my decision to take a gap year had led me to this moment, and I was forever grateful.

Here is a summary of the vision of this ministry, borrowed from youthalivetx.com:

> *Youth Alive North Texas is a strategic outreach organization that maintains the vision of reaching every student in every school across the region and beyond with the life-changing message of Jesus Christ. Youth Alive utilizes numerous strategies which combine the efforts of students, pastors and the Church. The central goal of these strategies is to empower students to be a light for Christ and reach their schools.*

> *Youth Alive is a grassroots movement led by Kyle and Janelle Embry and a diverse team of professional speakers, entertainers, media guys and college students. Several of the team members volunteer their time and resources to propel Youth Alive toward its vision of reaching this generation for Christ.*

> *Youth Alive's multi-faceted strategy can be summed up in one sentence: "Reaching students who are far from God while empowering students who are already believers to reach their schools."*

If you know Kyle, you know he is a bit crazy. He can be pretty intense at times, but he isn't the kind of guy who takes himself too seriously. He'll pull crazy stunts like preaching a youth service in full denim or a solid grey zookeeper uniform, or roll down his car window and yell random things at pedestrians—including, but not limited to, "I just got my colon cleansed!" and "I just found out I'm asexual!" (Hopefully, you can figure out which one of these is true!)

Kyle is a polarizing figure for some, but I can testify that his humility, passion, and love for God are all top-notch. I took note of many of the unique ways he would run his ministry. He needed a lot of help, but he wouldn't recruit just anyone; he wanted people who shared his vision and passion, and weren't just trying to use his platform to become big-time. He didn't hand me a mic and put me at center stage the moment I came on board, and I consistently watched him turn down experienced speakers who would ask to be a part of his work, because he felt like they were more interested in building their platforms than reaching students. He's the type of guy who will spend thirty minutes casting vision and two hours cleaning up after everyone else has gone home, and he's much more interested in building a team than hogging the spotlight. He tells it like it is and has a low tolerance for jackaroos, but at the end of the day, he genuinely cares and wants to invest in the leaders of tomorrow. This quote from Antoine de Saint-Exupery speaks to Kyle's strategy for developing leaders: "If you want to build a ship, don't drum up people to collect wood and don't assign them tasks and work, but rather teach them to long for the endless immensity of the sea."

I eventually transitioned out of Youth Alive as Maritza and I prepared to get married, as I prayerfully decided it would be best that I have more of a 9:00-5:00 job with less travel and a more stable income during our first few years of marriage. However, my time of serving alongside Kyle helped shape and form me into the man of God and minister of the Gospel that I am today. I discovered how important outreach and evangelism are in order for the local church to thrive. I learned how to network and obtain funding to help build a missions organization. I met some incredible people who were just as passionate about God as I was. I grew in my communication skills and learned how to build rapport with leaders who don't share my faith as we built relationships with principals and school administrators in order to help them solve problems their schools and this generation as a whole are facing. God did a lot through me, but, perhaps more importantly, He did a lot in me during my time with Youth Alive North Texas.

There are countless organizations in your community that are reaching people for Jesus, and hundreds of ways to get involved and make an impact for the Kingdom. All you have to do is a little leg work to find the one that aligns with your God-given vision and has room for the gifts He has given you.

No matter what stage of life you find yourself in, commit whatever you are doing to the Lord and fully invest your heart and soul in it. Find people who share your values, but are further along than you and can pour into your life as a mentor. God will develop your gifts and talents along the way; you don't have to wait until you have it all together to begin making a difference.

CHAPTER **11**

The Elijah Syndrome

In 1 Kings 18, Elijah has one of the most epic battles of Bible history. I'm sure you've heard of it—that time he defeated the prophets of Baal in an incredible "show and tell" moment on Mount Carmel.

If you want to set this book down to go read through the entire story, I won't be mad. It's one of my favorites, especially when illustrated by flannelgraph. However, the best part of the story is what happens next.

After the showdown, the wicked Queen Jezebel was extremely upset that her beloved prophets have been executed.

Understandable.

So she sent this message to Elijah: "Let the gods kill me if I fail to do to you what you did to my prophets by this time tomorrow" (see 1 Kings 19:2).

You would think Elijah—who was acting all big and bad just a few minutes ago—wouldn't be intimidated by the Queen's message. However, when he received it he quickly skipped town and hid out in the wilderness. At one point, he sat down under a tree and told the Lord it was probably about time he died.

You read that correctly—the man who had just won an epic victory against 450 false prophets is now terrified of one woman and wishes he were dead.

After saying his piece, Elijah fell asleep, but it wasn't long before he was awakened by an angel who told him to get up and eat.

Noticing that a cake and water had appeared next to him, Elijah quickly wolfed them down. But instead of getting up, he fell back into his slumber.

This caused the angel to return a second time. "Come on, lazybones! You need to get up while you still have the energy to embark on the journey that God has for you."

Elijah woke up and ate again before setting off for Horeb—aka Sinai, the mountain of God. He didn't eat anything for forty days or forty nights during this trip, so I guess it was good that he ate twice before he left. Once he arrived at Horeb, he found a cave and—you guessed it—fell asleep. While he was in the cave, the Lord spoke to him and asked, "Whatcha doin', Elijah?"

"Well, *Lord*," Elijah explained. As you know, I've been really loyal to you. But the rest of the Israelites are forsaking their covenants, tearing down your altars, and killing your prophets. I'm the only one left serving you, and now they're trying to kill me, too!"

I'm the only one serving you.

Sound familiar?

Many times, we as believers—even ministers—get discouraged and feel like no one else loves God as much as we do. Maybe our peers are on a different spiritual level, or we see churches doing things that don't seem "deep" enough, or we see so much craziness in the media that we're left feeling like there's no hope—the apocalypse is coming and we're the lone rangers left serving God by ourselves on an island surrounded by a sea of despair.

Just so you know, this mentality is 100 percent wrong.

I'm not sure where it comes from, but it gives me some level of hope to know that even Elijah fell prey to this mindset after a massive WIN. For him, it was a threat from a messenger of discouragement (i.e. Jezebel) that threw him off track, but sometimes we play this game entirely in our own minds—or someone says something that we blow way out of proportion in our inward dialogue.

After Elijah griped to God from the cave, the Lord responded in an interesting way. Let's pick up the story in 1 Kings 19:

And he [the Lord] said, "Go out and stand on the mount before the Lord." And behold, the Lord passed by, and a great and strong wind tore the mountains and broke in pieces the rocks before the Lord, but the Lord was not in the wind. And after the wind an earthquake, but the Lord was not in the earthquake. And after the earthquake a fire, but the Lord was not in the fire. And after the fire the sound of a low whisper [the NRSV calls it 'a sound of sheer silence' and the KJV calls it 'a still small voice']. And when Elijah heard it, he wrapped his face in his cloak and went out and stood at the entrance of the cave. And behold, there came a voice to him and said, "What are you doing here, Elijah?"
-1 Kings 19:11-13.

Interestingly enough, this is the same question God asked him in the cave.

Even more interesting, Elijah responded with the exact same spiel about how he's the only one serving God.

We can see the wind, see the fire, see the earth shake, and hear the still, small voice of God and still completely miss what He is trying to tell us. God responded to Elijah's discourse by ... completely ignoring it. Instead, He gave him a game plan, and it began with "Go back the way you came" (1 Kings 19:15).

Go back the way you came.

Sometimes, when we end up disillusioned, we get distracted from what God has called us to and end up hiding out in a cave of fear. It's not always a literal cave; it can be one we create in our own minds.

God told Elijah to anoint Hazael as king of Syria, Jehu as king of Israel, and Elisha as the prophet who Elijah would ultimately pass the baton to. He then shattered Elijah's pity party with one simple statement: "Hey stud, there are still 7,000 people left in Israel who don't worship Baal."

Seven thousand.

Elijah thought he was the only one, so he went and hid in a cave by himself—when he could have been back home, joining forces with seven thousand others who shared his vision.

My time with Youth Alive taught me that there's more to the story than meets the eye, and God is working behind the scenes in more ways than I think. There are times when I can be like Elijah, which causes me to miss out on what God is doing right in front of me.

I remember one of the first times I came down with a bad case of the Elijah Syndrome. This was before my Youth Alive days, when I was interning in the youth department at Heartland. I was visiting one of my youth ministry students for lunch at their high school. Since I arrived a few minutes early, I headed for the restroom before checking in as a visitor. Once there, I saw a couple of empty prescription drug bottles on the ground. I highly doubted the drugs formerly contained therein were actually being used for their prescribed purpose.

As I exited the restroom, it became apparent that the first lunch bell had rung, as students began to pour into the halls. I made my way toward the cafeteria to meet my student for lunch. Halfway there, I couldn't help but notice two kids making out in the hallway. They couldn't have been older than fifteen, but this wasn't a huge shock—except it was two girls who were making out.

I entered the cafeteria, my heart a little more broken for this generation than it had been fifteen minutes before. I know that hormones rage in high school students, and there's a ton of peer pressure, but it was heartbreaking that these things were taking place so openly and no one seemed to have a problem with it. I know we've barely scratched the surface of understanding what today's teenagers are dealing with, but it's still gut-wrenching to see so much confusion and mistreatment of God-given emotions and desires.

I sat with my student at his lunch table for twenty minutes, attempting to connect with him further and assist his quest to be a "missionary" to his school campus. These types of lunches are *always* awkward, no matter how extroverted or "youth-pastory" you are. We spent the first ten minutes talking about video games with the kid on our left, while the second ten minutes was spent talking to the kid on our right. He was raised in a Christian home and went to church, but was considering becoming an Atheist or Agnostic because he wasn't sure what to believe anymore and didn't want to cling to his parent's religion for no reason. I commended him for questioning these things—it's critical for students to find their own faith apart from their parents—but this conversation didn't seem to be very fruitful.

When the bell rang, signaling the end of lunch, I walked with my student to the door of his classroom in an attempt to encourage him in his faith and witness, which was the reason I had come to his school that day in the first place.

A few minutes later I was in my car, where I peeled the visitor's sticker off my shirt and stuck it to the steering wheel—as was my custom. I glanced down at it as I was pulling out of the parking lot. When I would leave a school, these stickers usually felt like a badge of honor, but today it just felt like a waste. I shook my head in discouragement. I felt like this school was a lost cause, even though it was located in a nice, suburban area with churches on every corner.

I didn't feel like praying, but I was able to whimper a few words— much like Elijah in the cave. "God, there's no one that cares about these students except for me! How am I supposed to make an impact at this school? What I'm doing isn't working."

When I began serving with Youth Alive a short time later, I quickly learned that there were far more than seven thousand people in the Dallas/Fort Worth Metroplex alone who were faithfully serving God and reaching the next generation with the Gospel. There are countless stories all around us that we just haven't heard yet, and perhaps one of the reasons why we haven't heard these stories is because the people who hold them don't view them as significant moments, or they haven't yet developed the courage to tell their stories and tell them well.

We are called to pass the baton. The baton is not our logo, our
values, nor our movement; it is the Gospel of Jesus Christ.
-Phillip Pretorius

CHAPTER 12

To The Church at DFW

I really like how the Apostle Paul begins his letters, many of which became books in our New Testament. [7]

To the saints who are in Ephesus, and are faithful in Christ Jesus.
To all the saints in Christ Jesus who are at Philippi .
To the churches of Galatia.
To the church of God that is in Corinth.

Paul begins each letter by addressing the Church—the community of believers—in a given geographical location. He doesn't address his letters to a senior pastor, a deacon's committee, or a church board—but to the congregation as a whole. He then writes to instruct, encourage, correct, and answer specific questions he had been asked in their letters to him. While the content of each letter is different, there is one common thread throughout: Paul highlights the work of God in a precise location.

I think all of us need to be reminded of the work of God that is taking place all around us. None of us are the "only ones" serving God, and there is far more happening behind the scenes than we could wrap our minds around. I'm sure Paul's letters barely scratched the surface of all God was doing in those communities in his day, but he gave us a glimpse into how the Kingdom was coming to Ephesus, Philippi, Galatia, Corinth, and other places where the first-century Church was being established.

Today, I want to give a small glimpse into what I've seen God do in my own community, in twenty-first century North Texas. Most of these stories are from the time I spent serving with Youth Alive, and capture the work of God in the lives of otherwise ordinary, high school students. I'm in no way equating my experiences to Scripture, but instead sharing where I've seen God at work to both inspire and encourage you to begin writing your own story of how God is moving in your community.

Sarah was a high school student from the Fort Worth suburb of Burleson. I first met her when she attended a Youth Alive training day for students who desired to become "campus missionaries" who would reach their school with the Gospel.

On one occasion, Sarah told me that she had met a girl in the cafeteria during lunch. Her parents were involved in witchcraft and she herself claimed to be a Wiccan as her religion. On the day they met, this girl told Sarah that all of her friends had abandoned her because of this.

In her email to me, Sarah stated that she began praying for her on a regular basis. This went on for two months. One day, the girl came up to Sarah and told her that two of her friends had been banned from hanging out with her—their parents did not want them to spend time around a Wiccan. Sarah responded by telling her that she would always be there for her and continued to pray.

The very next day, another student told Sarah that the Wiccan girl was looking for her. When their paths crossed, the girl asked Sarah to tell her about her God. Sarah told her about creation, the fall, and how Jesus can restore us to our original design, and went on to share a bit about how her faith had helped her in her own life. "I didn't even sweat," Sarah recalled. "The words just flowed though my lips; it was definitely the Holy Sprit speaking [through me]."

When Sarah finished sharing the Gospel, her friend responded: "Okay, I want to accept Christ right before our first period. Can we do this before the first period?" She then remarked that she wanted to cry, because she felt the presence of God.

Whoa!

I emailed her back saying, "Sarah, you are insane!"

"I hope that's a good thing," she replied. "What do you mean, *insane*?"

"Yes, it's a good thing!" I said in my follow-up email. I mean bold—insane for Jesus! I haven't heard of any other students praying for Wiccans at their school. We talk about deliverance, freedom ministry, the power of God—but at the end of the day, I don't see a whole lot of people *actually* doing this, much less at their high school!

Here we have a teenager—not a Bible school graduate, a teenager—who is actively "doing the stuff" and making an impact in her community. If I were the Apostle Paul writing about the work of God in DFW, I couldn't help but share that story—but there is no way I would have known to share it without Sarah first sharing it with me!

Do you see how important it is to tell your story?

Who knows how many people reading this book will be inspired by Sarah's story and end up doing something else to make God's Kingdom a reality in their city; all because Sarah first did it and had the courage to tell her story, and I had the courage to write this book in an effort to tell my story and the stories of those I've come into contact with.

We often don't share our stories, because we think it's more "humble" to keep them on the down-low, but for every story we keep locked inside, there are lives that are not being impacted and potentially reached with the Gospel, and Sarah's story is just the tip of the iceberg.

Around this same time, another story ran across my desk that involved a young man by the name of Dan. He lived on the north side of DFW, and was a junior at his high school. He had been raised in a godly home and attended church his entire life, but was just now being convicted about being more public with his faith. He realized his peers, and even his friends, knew little about the very real relationship with Christ he had, and he became determined to change that. Even though we live in the Bible Belt, it's easy to go through the motions and just be a "good person" while keeping your story of God's transformative power hidden behind a more socially acceptable front.

The funny thing about this story was that Dan was an introvert—not the type of guy who you would expect to make a big impact when it comes to evangelism. Still, he felt compelled to do something to share his faith, even if that meant starting small.

Dan finally mustered up enough courage to place it on his desk during first period, something we challenge students to do through Youth Alive. He read a few verses before class started, but when the bell rang, he closed his Bible and positioned it on the upper left corner of his desk instead of returning it to his backpack.

As one of his fellow classmates was heading to his own desk, he saw the Bible sitting on the corner of Dan's desk and scoffed. *What is this, a scene from some cheesy, Christian movie?*

"Dude, is that a *BIBLE*?" the kid sneered at Dan.

"Why yes, it is," Dan calmly replied. "I'm a Christian and this book has changed my life."

"Whatever," the kid retorted. "My mom says it's a load of crap. Religion hasn't done anything for anyone. It's full of worthless myths, and the Bible is no exception. She says it's a waste of time and money to pay attention to it."

I find it interesting that this student didn't seem to have his own opinion on the matter; he could only repeat what he heard his mom say.

Dan was a bit taken aback. He hadn't anticipated being mocked this severely after doing something as simple as discreetly placing his Bible on his desk. "Well ..." he began, clearing his throat. "I don't know your mom, and don't mean any disrespect to her, but that's simply not true. This book tells the story of Jesus—who was God—coming down to restore relationship with us. It's not a waste of time, and it's not just my 'religion;' Jesus has changed my life." [8]

The kid shrugged this off and made his way to his desk with little response. It was clear that he wasn't in the mood to have an actual discussion; he was just spouting off what he had heard at home.

Dan was a bit rattled from this encounter, taken aback by the level of intensity of this random confrontation. He took a deep breath and settled back in his chair as he awaited the beginning of class. The rest of the morning passed without any further intense exchanges. However, when lunch came, the kid from earlier approached Dan in the cafeteria.

"I can't stop thinking about what you said earlier; how convinced you are that the Bible is true. Can we talk more about this?"

The two students ended up having lunch together that day. They went on to meet on several more occasions as Dan shared his faith with his classmate in a conversational and relational manner. For this student—who had never heard the Gospel—Dan was his window to God, offering a different perspective than what his mom was feeding him at home.

This student ended up surrendering his life to Christ at lunch one day and he attended church with Dan a few times. While I don't know where his story went from there, I know that the simple act of Dan placing a Bible on his desk (even though he was afraid to do so) made an eternal impact in the life of at least one student.

Another North Texas high school junior who made an impact at her school was Beth. One day, she was on the way back from a match with her volleyball team. They had won, so an upbeat sense of excitement filled the bus. Several of her teammates already knew about her faith— Beth wasn't the quiet, reserved type. Although she hadn't stood up in the locker room and preached to her entire team, many of her peers were aware that she had a vibrant relationship with God.

On this trip, however, Beth began to feel a burden and urgency. It troubled her that many of her teammates knew about her faith, but she had not gone any further; she had not challenged them with a call to action. So, she began a conversation with another girl and, naturally, several other girls within earshot made themselves part of the conversation. Over the next two hours, Beth ended up leading eleven of her teammates to the Lord! This did not happen during a church service or campus Bible study, but on the bus on the way home from a volleyball match—all because one girl had the courage to share her story and invite others to join The Story as well.

● ● ●

Sarah, Dan, and Beth were students who were impacted by the ministry of Youth Alive. As I talked about in Chapter 8, we would do assemblies (where I would reveal that I was a 22-year-old virgin) in public schools. These assemblies were secular in nature, in accordance with laws prohibiting school administrators from promoting any one religion over another. This is why we would come alongside local churches to equip students like Sarah, Dan, and Beth. We can't share Jesus during school hours, but *they* can. We found that this was the best way to impact the schools—by encouraging students to reach students in a relational manner without force or coercion.

This played out in a number of ways; the ministry was very multi-faceted and grassroots. One of our biggest and most exciting outreaches was called *Seven Projects*. Essentially, this involved bringing multiple churches together to impact an entire community. This required weeks, months, and sometimes even years of groundwork, but it would all begin with relationships. When we would connect well with a youth pastor in any given city, we would serve them in any way we could—through resourcing, youth services, student training days, and the Seven Project.

Due to the large amount of bullying and violence facing public schools today, each school is required to have a certain number of all-school assemblies each year that cover a variety of topics and are given the funding necessary to bring in a speaker to do the assembly. Most of these school assembly speakers are believers, primarily because few care about the condition of our schools as much as Christians (the schools pay for the assemblies, but not much; it's not a good use of time from a strictly business standpoint). The all-school assemblies are 100% secular in their content, but the assembly speaker will often partner with a student-led faith community to host a second event outside of school hours (which often gives the speaker a chance to receive a second honorarium from a church in order to cover all of their expenses and make a somewhat decent living). This event will usually take place at night, and will sometimes be off school property at a nearby church. Other times, space will be rented from the school district in an auditorium, cafeteria, gymnasium, or on the football field. This is a "win" for the school, as the assembly is paid for by earmarked funds and they have the chance to receive an additional rental fee that they can use for whatever they desire.

As you probably guessed, a Seven Project would combine the daytime assemblies with the nighttime event. But we wouldn't stop there. Instead of working with a single Christian club on campus or a single church in the community, our local contact (who was typically the youth pastor at the local church within our denomination) would reach out to other churches in the city, with the goal of multiple churches partnering together to share the vision, expense, and fruit of the outreach.

Once we confirmed an assembly with school administrators, we would begin partnering with churches across the city for seven weeks of planning and promotion. This would be a joint effort between our team and the local contacts. We would provide resources, guidance, and encouragement, but the bulk of the planning would be done by the local churches. This was because we understood that we would be long gone the day after the event, but the local churches would be the boots on the ground to follow-up and steward the long-term impact. We would sometimes travel to the city for individual or multi-church youth services in the weeks before the event, but we usually just showed up the night before with our team.

The day of the Seven Project, we would do as many assemblies as possible at local middle and high schools—with as many as five assemblies back-to-back with little time for breaks or lunch. There would even be times when we would set up our equipment (which would take an hour or two; it was *much* more equipment than other assembly speakers that would just plug in a mic and start talking) the night before at the high school, do an assembly in the morning, move everything over to the middle school, eat lunch, do an assembly at the middle school, then move everything back to the high school for the night service.

For the assemblies, we brought in truss to build a ten-foot set and DJ booth complete with screens, projects, and lights, and wheeled in our own high-capacity sound system that would blow the socks off the students in the front row. There would be times when students would walk in with zero expression on their faces, as they would rather be in class than listen to some guy ramble for half an hour, but they would immediately get excited when they heard the loud music and saw our sweet setup and Heavy G—our amazing DJ with a lively personality.

Since we were intentionally trying to avoid being the old guy droning on for half an hour, we would tell very stripped-down versions of our life messages that could fit neatly in a window of under ten minutes. Often, we would utilize the night service to tell more of the story that there simply was not time to talk about during the day.

At the end of the assembly, with the principal's permission, a few students would take the mic and invite the student body back to the faith-based, night event. We would typically have free food and giveaways to attract students, but we did not rely on this alone to pack the room. Instead, during the seven weeks of planning, the local churches would recruit students from their youth groups to be our "street team"—they would give them t-shirts and graphics, and spread the word in the community before we ever showed up. In small communities, Seven Project would often be the talk of the town for several months.

For the night event, we would have bounce houses, mechanical bulls, car bashes, live music, and more. There would also be free food and giveaways like Xboxes and iPads, but there would be times when we would use donated gift cards to be more budget friendly. The local churches would share the cost, and once a budget was put together, we would determine how much we could do. Some events were simple and operated on shoestring budgets of a few hundred dollars, while others pushed the ten thousand-dollar mark. We would host these activities in the school parking lot, and after an hour or so of fun, we would begin the service in the school gym or auditorium. This service would look a little different than the daytime services. For starters, it was evangelistic in nature and the Gospel was clearly presented with an altar call following. It would also revolve around one, primary speaker. I would occasionally be the speaker who preached the Gospel, but I would usually just share for a few minutes and Kyle would deliver the longer message and call to faith. This would be my favorite part of the night, as I stood backstage out of audience view and looked on. I was almost always left in tears as I watched several hundred students respond to the Gospel, streaming to the front of the room where adult volunteers from the local churches would pray with them (many of these people were in tears as well; it was always a powerful moment for everyone involved).

During my window, I would pick up my story where I had left off earlier in the day. For example, if I had previously shared about being a 22-year-old virgin to talk about non-religious abstinence, I would switch gears at night since it was a faith-based setting. I would go a little deeper with my story and talk about how Jesus calls us to live our lives set apart, and how I was personally set free from my struggle with pornography.

Though the planning was similar, no two Seven Projects were ever the same. The specifics would always be tailored to the school and individual churches and we would see God do something different each time.

One particular Seven Project that I was involved in stands out strongly to this day. In this city, there were six churches that came together—two Baptist churches, a Methodist church, a Lutheran church, a Catholic church, and an Assembly of God church. We usually met with the staff and volunteers from each church seven and three weeks out, just to make sure everything was firing on all cylinders. This event was no different, so one Sunday evening we made the three-hour drive to this city to nail down some logistics and assign volunteer roles for the night service. We were sitting around a large, round table with all of the youth leaders of the various churches, determining who would take ownership of the different assignments. The Catholics would handle the food, one of the Baptist guys would purchase the giveaway items, and so forth. As we were going through the list, the Lutheran youth minister spoke up.

"Hey guys, I don't mind helping out with food or giveaways or whatever, but I don't know about all this altar call stuff. I don't know if I want our guys to be involved in that part of the service."

The rest of us slowly looked at one another, trying not to make it obvious what we were doing.

The Lutheran minister continued, "Feel free to assign me whatever you feel is best. I'm sure it's a great event, but I'm not comfortable with an altar call."

Unsure how to respond in the moment, we dropped the issue and moved on to the other stages of planning. But as we were driving home that night, we knew we could not change the structure of the event based upon one person's feedback—the altar call is an integral part of the Seven Project night service.

Romans 10:9 says "... if you confess with your mouth that Jesus is Lord and believe in your heart that God raised him from the dead, you will be saved."

We wanted to give every student a chance to confess Jesus as Lord. We didn't just want to give them a cupcake or have them fill out a card and wait to speak with a minister at a church; we wanted them to be able to receive Jesus at their school and bring the church to them. Though it was surprising to see a youth minister who didn't value this portion of the night service, we all wanted to move in the same direction together, so we put him in charge of another area where he was more comfortable. We didn't make a big deal out of the situation or give him a lecture on why we thought altar calls were important. Instead, we saw value in the fact that he wanted to join forces with fellow believers from very different backgrounds than his own in order to make a difference in the city, which in itself is worth uniting around.

When the night service took place a short time later, everything went exactly as planned. There were more than seven hundred students in attendance, which was about what we expected based on the numbers from the daytime assemblies, and the level of energy in the gymnasium was high. Everyone loved the food, the students were having fun playing the games, the volunteers were charismatic and engaging, and the local [family-friendly] rapper who was slated to perform before the service showed up on time. I personally did not expect much from a skinny, white guy moonlighting as a Christian rapper, but the crowd seemed to really like him and it was a good transition between the activities and speaking. Myself and another guy spoke briefly, which went well. The students seemed to be attentive and it's honestly more fun to preach to a bunch of rowdy teenagers in a high school gym than it is to preach to a bunch of religious folks in church.

After we spoke, Kyle delivered the core message and closed out the evening with a passionate altar call. As his message drew to a close, he called all of the youth ministers and volunteer leaders to stand in a line in front of him. "We live three hours away!" Kyle exclaimed, "But these folks are all right here in your city! They care about you, they live the message I'm preaching, and they are here for you when you need them."

This was key, because we honestly did not want to be the "heroes" of the night. We had made a solid connection and established trust throughout the day, but we knew we couldn't be the ones these students depended on day in and day out. While a local youth leader from a small-town church may not be able to deliver a high-energy message like Kyle did, they are available to walk with students through the ups and downs of life in ways he cannot due to his position, which is why Kyle wanted the local leaders to take center stage as the Gospel was proclaimed.

As usual, I found a corner to duck into and pray as the altar call was given, knowing that some of these students were hearing a complete Gospel message for the very first time. As Kyle appealed to the crowd to surrender their lives to Jesus, I looked up and noticed someone standing in the line of leaders waiting to pray with any students who responded.

It was the Lutheran youth minister.

He was participating in the altar call.

This was the same guy who had theological issues with us even doing this, and had not been shy about sharing them during our planning meeting. His church "doesn't do altar calls"—yet there he was at the front of the high school gym, ready to rumble.

As Kyle began to build to the climax of the call to faith, I was still in a state of shock and disbelief. I kept my eye on this minister, wondering if he planned on piggybacking on another leader. You know—prayer piggybacking. Okay, maybe you don't know what this means, but it's very common in the church world. In order to prayer piggyback, all you have to do is stand slightly behind a person who is praying for someone, rest your hand on that person's back, squint your eyes and nod your head, and you're home free while the person in front of you does all the "work." We've all done that; I know I have! I wasn't trying to judge this Lutheran guy or be cynical about the moment, but I genuinely wondered if this was what he planned on doing since he was so adamantly against this portion of the evening from the very beginning.

As students began to respond, I quickly realized that this was not the case; he was in it to win it. He stood by himself in the lineup of leaders as hundreds of students rushed to the altar. We had planned for two or three hundred to respond, but it soon became apparent that more than *ninety* percent of the crowd had emptied out onto the gym floor.

I began to weep, knowing how special this moment was. Not only was it one of the largest responses in the history of Youth Alive North Texas (in terms of percentage), but the Lutheran minister had decided to participate in the best part of the evening. Students from his church lined up in front of him—the guy who insisted that he did not "do" altar calls—waiting to receive prayer from their leader. He knelt with dozens of students as they surrendered their lives to Jesus, one after another.

When God begins to move in people's hearts, denominational lines and theological differences don't matter nearly as much as we think they do, and a leader from a church that doesn't believe in altar calls begins to weep and embrace those who are being raised to life in Christ—on the gym floor of their high school. This is what it was all about for our team, and I think this guy took hold of our vision. In that moment, his theology and questions took a back seat to what God was doing right in front of him.

● ● ●

You don't have to travel far to see a mission field. Short-term, overseas mission trips are life-changing and fantastic experiences, but each day, our young people step foot in a difficult and challenging context—the public high school, America's unreached mission field that seems to be hidden in plain sight.

One youth pastor at a small church in Fort Worth began intentionally focusing on encouraging his students to see their school through this lens—that it truly is a mission field and that they are called to be salt and light on their campus. It's tricky, as pastors, youth ministers, and school administrators cannot bring the message of the Gospel to public campuses, however, students CAN!

One group of four friends caught the vision their pastor was casting, and were burdened with a contagious passion that led them to join forces to reach the goal of saturating each middle and high school across our regional area with the Gospel. On Monday morning, they asked a few of their teachers if they could share something about their faith with the classes before the class time actually started. Remarkably, they got the green light! They split up into two pairs of two and went throughout their classes that week, sharing their personal testimonies and preaching the gospel—one classroom at a time!

Here's the fun part. In the course of one week, they led twenty-three classmates to the Lord!

These were *students*. Not youth pastors. Not senior pastors. Students. Students who grasped how much power there was in being campus missionaries where they were planted. They understood the power of story, and God moved mightily when they shared theirs.

I hope you see the value in ordinary people sharing their stories. (Even high school students can do it!) My prayer is that this will inspire you to share your own story. It's amazing what can happen when an otherwise ordinary person encounters God and tells a few people about it. After all, isn't this the commission Jesus left us with?

The Youth Alive team in North Texas has written a book entitled *Hidden in Plain Sight: America's Unreached Mission Field*. This book will tell you more about their vision and offer practical advice to make an impact in your community. I highly recommend this book for those involved in student ministry and anyone who is passionate about reaching the next generation. For more information, please visit www.youthalivetx.com or search for the book on Amazon.

CHAPTER 13

Billy Twitters and His Blue Whale Problem

A few years ago, I made the decision to be a person who is constantly looking to improve themselves and continue their education. I want to be someone who always seeks to grow and be developed in every area of my life. I have wholeheartedly embraced this concept over the past few years, and have set goals to "feed" myself in a variety of ways.

Since 2011, I've maintained a strict minimum of reading *at least* twelve, non-fiction books per year. The topics vary from spirituality and theology to business and finance, and I have, of course, continued my reading of the only Book that has stood the test of time (i.e. the Bible).

I also subscribe to several podcasts. I listen to people who I feel mirror my beliefs, people I rarely agree with, and people who simply interest me with what they have to say.

One of my favorite ways to continue my education as of late has been listening to TED Talks. For the longest time, I had no clue what *TED* meant, but I loved the dynamic range of speakers and topics.

If you're not familiar with TED Talks, they are conferences and events where expert communicators share concepts and ideas from their fields with a live audience. These talks are video recorded on DVDs and distributed across the globe via the Internets. The massive, online library of talks is continually growing, and features topics like nuclear physics, the AIDS epidemic, wages for women in the workplace, and everything in-between.

TED actually stands for *Technology, Entertainment, and Design.* Growing up, I was the kind of kid who always wanted to take things apart to find out how they worked, so I naturally gravitate toward the things discussed in TED talks.

Typically, I watch a couple of talks each month. I listen to what is said, write down anything I feel is relevant to my life or anything I can learn from, and move on. But once in a while, something is said that is so compelling that it remains in the forefront of my mind and I discuss it with people around me.

Not too long ago, I watched a talk that was like that. Mac Barnett, a children's book author, was discussing the fiction-writing process. You can probably find it online if you want to watch the full talk, so I won't give it all away here, but he said a few things in particular that stood out to me.

> *There's a secret power that fictional authors possess. The best books have a way of blurring the lines between the world of fiction and reality. For instance, we know that Sherlock Holmes is not a real character, but for some reason, people flock to the fake address of his home in England, and we embrace him as if he were real. Or, when we read about Narnia, every wardrobe (or closest door) we see suddenly has the power to lead us to a secret, magical world.*

Mac went on to tell us how he loves writing for children, because they are quicker to accept that something make believe could in fact become a reality. Children are often willing to ponder the *what if's* that adults are quick to dismiss.

One of the first books Mac wrote was titled *Billy Twitters and His Blue Whale Problem*. In this fictional story, Billy was given a blue whale for a pet—as a punishment.

When Billy Twitters fails to clean his room, brush his teeth, and eat his peas, his parents spring into action. They purchase him a blue whale that arrives via *FedUp*, a courier service that specializes in *Delivering Punishment Worldwide*. Billy is expected to care for his new pet—which ends up being quite a chore—especially when he has to gather thousands of krill each evening to feed his new friend dinner. The illustrations in the book are remarkable, and include a word-free, two-page spread of Billy furiously pedaling his bike with a whale in-tow on a skateboard, taking out telephone poles and traffic signals along the way. Later on, Billy is uninvited from a pool party when the host learns that he would have to bring his pet whale with him. Finally, after cleaning out the whale's large, stinky mouth, Billy decides that it would make a good place to live and moves in. A strange ending to a strange story, but it has a certain magic about it that delights children, while adults roll their eyes in the background.

What an interesting mind Mac must have in order to create such a compelling tale.

This was the first thing that came to my mind after hearing Mac discuss his book, which was written back in 2009.

Billy Twitters and His Blue Whale Problem is a perfect example of the best kind of fiction, because it seamlessly blends an outlandish tale with reality. Parents appreciate that it includes true facts about whales woven into the fun story that their kids love. The book got great reviews, which is no surprise to me. Not only is the story fresh and unique, the attention to detail in the illustrations is incredible. Mac's illustrator went as far as drawing vintage turn-of-the-century scenes in the front and back of the book in which fictional vendors advertised various period, sailing items to add a "fantasy meets reality" element to the story.

The most inquisitive minds that peeked behind the book's dust jacket found an even more enticing advertisement. No doubt invoking disbelief from their parents, children stumbled upon a mail-order certificate for the unthinkable: a 30-day risk free, no obligation ...

... blue whale!

Seriously? A blue whale?

That's a joke, right?

Is that even possible?

Could you imagine being five years old and stumbling across something like that? You've just finished reading a tale that sucked you into the world of Billy Twitters and his problem of blue whale ownership. Your mind is racing with thoughts of what it would be like to have your own blue whale—in the neighborhoods of San Francisco. And suddenly, you're presented with the opportunity to discover this exciting and terrible reality for yourself.

What would you do?

Believe it or not, kids sent these mail-order certificates in.

During his TED talk, Mac showed a photo of an actual letter he received. Scrawled in green crayon are the words, "Dear people, I bet you ten bucks you won't send me a blue whale! Elliot Gannon, Age 6."

In reality, Elliot (and every other kid that sent in the certificate) did receive something in return: a long, detailed letter that outlined the complications of the situation. The sender? A "Norwegian Law Firm" by the name of *Magnusson, Olafsson, & Oskarsdottir*.

"Dear Elliot," the letter read. "We regret to inform you that due to a sudden change in Norwegian customs law, we are currently unable to ship your blue whale (Reference #: 34552900). Your whale, whose name is Eugene, is being held in Sognefjord, which we can assure you is a very comfortable and appealing place for a blue whale to live."

The letter continues to amaze with a bout of wit, personalized to each individual kid who sent in the certificate. For example, in the letter to Elliot Gannon, the "lawyer" writes about how tempting the bet of $10 USD is, but gambling under such circumstances would get his firm in trouble with the Norwegian authorities.

"A team of lawyers is working day and night to find a way to get your blue whale to you," the letter goes on to say. "In the meantime, we are pleased to enclose this photograph of Eugene, which is suitable for framing."

If that isn't enough for you, it gets better.

"And you can leave Eugene a message on his personal answering machine by calling this number. We're sure he'd be glad to hear from you! On behalf of our client, Blue Whale Direct, we thank you for your interest in owning a blue whale, and apologize for this inconvenience."

You better believe that any kid who has gotten this far in the process is going to call in and leave a message for their whale. When they dial the number, they get an answering machine with a series of whale sounds, followed by a familiar beep.

One of the first kids to call in was a young boy by the name of Nikko, whose whale's name was Randolph. The first message he left went something like this: "Hello, this is Nikko! I'm your owner, Randolph! Hello! So, this is the first time I can ever talk to you, and I might talk to you soon, another day! Bye!"

Over the course of the next four years, Nikko called more than twenty-five times. He asked Randolph what he was doing, wished him a Merry Christmas—you know, the kind of things you say to your pet whale. Sometimes, he would call back several times a day to talk to Randolph about his grandparents, school, and crossword puzzles.

When you listen to Nikko's messages, which Mac shares in his TED talk, you can hear the joy and sincerity in his voice as he talks to his very own blue whale. It seems as if he truly believed that Randolph was actually his and they would soon be together. Because of this, he poured his childlike heart out to him in a series of voice messages.

Some might say that this is a cruel joke; others might say that Nikko is incredibly naive, but Mac calls him "the best reader he could hope for," because he's the type of reader who isn't afraid to blur the lines between fiction and reality.

Regardless of where you stand, I think there's more to this story than meets the eye; there's something here that we can take in, reflect on, and perhaps even learn from.

At that time the disciples came to Jesus, saying, "Who is the greatest in the kingdom of heaven?" And calling to him a child, he put him in the midst of them and said, "Truly, I say to you, unless you turn and become like children, you will never enter the kingdom of heaven. Whoever humbles himself like this child is the greatest in the kingdom of heaven. -Matthew 18:1-4

There seems to be a profound significance in approaching the Kingdom of God with the heart posture of a child—carrying an attitude of awe and wonder, without an ounce of cynicism. It's as if that's where our lives begin, but we're slowly pulled away from the place of childlike faith, trust, and dependence as we grow older.

Children take your word for it. They have no problem trusting Jesus when He says things like, "If you speak to the mountain and command it to be cast into the sea, it will be done for you" (Mark 11:23, Matthew 21:21). When did we, as adults, stop living life this way?

Somewhere along the line, we got cynical.

We learned to doubt.

We learned that it's not safe to trust.

We chose the way of disappointment over the way of hope.

We closed off a part of our hearts that was once open to childlike wonder.

Nikko *really* believed that he was getting a blue whale.

As crazy as it seems, he took the ad's word for it.

He didn't doubt.

It was 100% possible in his world.

I know this is just a silly story about a blue whale, but ...

When did we stop doing this with God?

When did we stop taking Him at His word?

When did we stop believing that He can and does do the impossible—the literal impossible, not just the things we think are difficult?

It's already crazy enough that we believe in a God we can't see or touch or feel—what if we actually started believing He is who He says He is?

Just a thought.

It's A Christmas Miracle!

S hortly after we got married, my wife and I experienced a series of events that gave us an entirely new perspective in a major area of our lives—we learned that when God makes a promise, He actually follows through with it.

The series of events that we experienced didn't just happen; they began with a few key steps of action and faith.

These events that I'm referring to have to do with money.

Yes, these next few chapters are about tithing.

But they're also about so much more than that.

Before you skip this section entirely, let me assure you that I have no axe to grind. I'm not in a position to benefit or suffer from your decision to tithe or not to tithe. I don't pastor a church, I don't have a 501c3, and I won't think any less of you if you think what I have to say is total bull. I would, however, like to share our story with you.

So here it goes ...

It began with a study of Malachi 3:10, which the church we were attending at the time was doing.

Bring the full tithe into the storehouse, that there may be food in my house. And thereby put me to the test, says the LORD of hosts, if I

will not open the windows of heaven for you and pour down for you a
*blessing until there is no more need. -*Malachi 3:10

God offers a pretty strong challenge here. After all, where else in the
Scriptures does He invite us to test Him?

It's almost as if He's inviting us to a life of generosity—a life of open
hands and open hearts.

It's almost as if He's beckoning us to recapture a little piece of our
childlike innocence.

It's almost as if He's inviting us to trust Him again.

The truth is, God isn't after your money—He's after your heart.

So doesn't it make since that He'd go after the thing that most often
grabs ahold of our hearts, the thing that most often pushes Him to
second place?

I think it does.

Can you hear the gentle whisper of the Father who knows you and
wants the best for you?

You can take My word for it. I won't let you down. Go ahead, put Me to
the test and see what happens.

After all, what have you really got to lose?

Maritza and I experienced three major milestones on our journey
of taking God at His word in regard to tithing. These key moments
helped change our perspective on everything. There have been other
factors, of course; I don't know if I could retrace every ripple that led
us to where we are now.

Now, I know what you might be thinking here.

Not once does the idea of giving 10% appear in the New Testament.

I've heard that one before, and I have an answer for it. If you'd like
to discuss it, be my guest and shoot me an email.

● ● ●

It began in a garden—an Olive Garden.

Well, not really—that just sounded like a fun thing to say about the first milestone, since it's probably the last place you would expect a pivotal moment to take place.

In reality, the story began in our upbringings. Both Maritza and I were raised in Christian homes. Although our individual families had their fair share of problems, they were both very safe and healthy environments overall. We both grew up in church and we both learned about the importance of tithing all the way back in Sunday School.

Back then, it was all very cut and dry. Ten cents of every dollar went straight to the church, no questions asked. We save, we tithe, and we go beyond that to bless others as we are able. This was a core value in our lives as children, and it's a core value in our lives today as well. But just because we grew up this way, doesn't mean we never struggled with doubt.

For us, tithing was just part of the drill. The "why" behind the action wasn't 100% real to us. It was simply another thing we did, another thing our parents had passed on to us, which we both made the choice to embrace after we left home. We never really stopped to ask ourselves *why* we did it, and I don't think you could say our hearts were overflowing with the kind of radical generosity that God invites us to when He invites us to put Him first in our finances.

But that was back before any of this happened.

The first milestone on our journey took place while we were dating. Well, actually, there was one summer when we had broken up—with the intention of being done for good. Long story short, we felt the relationship needed to go in different directions and we were no longer together. I was spending five weeks working as the media guy for a youth summer camp, and I was conflicted. I had emotionally detached from the relationship to the point of throwing out pictures, letters, any item that reminded me of her. It was over and I was "over it." But as

I talked with God while working at the camp, He would speak to me about Maritza.

Finally, I messaged her on Facebook (real romantic, I know) and told her that I had been wrestling with some thoughts that I wanted to share with her. I asked if she would be open to talk over a classy meal at Olive Garden when I got a day off.

The actual invite went something like this: *Hey, I'd like to talk and I would enjoy your company. If you want a free lunch, meet me @ Grapevine OG at 1:00 pm Wednesday. I'll be there, even if you don't show up.*

Real romantic, right? How could she resist such seductive words?

She did show up on that particular Wednesday at 1:00 pm, perhaps only because Olive Garden was one of her favorite restaurants. We reconnected, talked about our summers, and shared what we felt God was speaking to us about the state of our relationship. It was fantastic.

As we finished eating, our server, Rocio, came by to grab the check. Before she got away, I asked, "Can you do me a huge favor? When you come back with my card, can you also bring back a prayer request so we can pray for you?" This may seem a bit cheesy, but it was something we just felt prompted to do, and was a common occurrence when we would go out to eat.

Rocio seemed a bit confused. She walked away in silence, and had a different server return my credit card. Confused, but unoffended, Maritza and I assumed that she just didn't want us to pray for her. Little did we know, in reality, she was so overwhelmed by our random act of kindness toward her that she didn't know how to respond.

As we were preparing to leave, Rocio approached our table.

"I don't understand. What are you asking me to do for you?"

Maritza explained to her in Spanish that we were Christians who loved Jesus, and simply wanted to know if there was any area of her life where she needed prayer.

We would later learn that no one had ever asked if they could pray for her.

Rocio closed her eyes as her head fell. When she looked back up at us, her eyes were watery. It was then that she began to tell us her story.

"I just had a baby a few months ago, making me a mother of three. Right after the baby was born, my husband walked out on me and my kids, and now I am the sole provider. I am working two jobs, and having a lot of trouble making ends meet. My mom was helping me take care of the kids during the day while I worked, but she just passed away a couple of weeks ago. I have no one left to help me raise my kids."

We were a bit caught off guard, but it was what she said next that really shocked us.

"A few days ago, the doctor informed me that I have cancer."

Our hearts sank. It was one of those gut-wrenching stories, the kind that make you long for a better ending. We were unsure of how she had even been able to make it to work that morning, unsure of how she was able to wait tables and hold herself together.

Fighting back tears, Maritza told Rocio that Jesus loved her, and that we were going to ask Him to enter into her story. Right there, in the corner of Olive Garden, we joined hands, bowed our heads, and called upon Jesus.

After we parted ways, Maritza couldn't get Rocio off of her mind.

"I felt so small and helpless, when all I wanted to do was help her," she would later tell me.

As time went on, Maritza continued to pray for Rocio. One morning in particular, the burden she felt was even stronger. "I began to weep and weep and weep so heavily for her," she told me. "It was as though I could feel her pain, her fears, her heartache. I knew I couldn't do everything I wanted to do for her, but I had to do something."

Maritza and I went to Walmart and purchased a gift card for Rocio, so that she could buy groceries for herself and her children. We also got her a beautiful greeting card that had an inscription about how God is always with us, even in the hard times. This was all we could afford at the time, and it seemed so small compared to how great her need was.

Maritza went on to submit Rocio's story to 94.9 KLTY, a Christian radio station in DFW that does a *Christmas Wish* program, where they match people in need with people who are willing to step in and meet the need. We were hopeful, but weren't completely sure she would be chosen. There are dozens of sad stories that come flooding in, a picture of the extreme heartache that often plagues people during the holidays.

It wasn't long before Maritza got a call from a group of people who attended Watermark Church in Dallas. They told her that Rocio's story had caught their eye. They had just begun meeting as a formal, small group of the church, and God had laid it on their hearts to reach out to someone in need, rather than simply being an "us-four-and-no-more" type of small group. As Bob Goff would say, "They went from being just a Bible-study to a Bible-doing."

The leader of the small group invited us and Rocio to a special meeting at one of the member's houses.

It was a chilly night as we began the long drive to the other side of town. We met up with Rocio, and she followed us to an elaborate, upper-middle-class neighborhood in North Dallas. As we got out of our cars and made our way up the front walk, we had no clue what to expect.

We entered the house to find the only thing more warm and inviting than the gorgeous decor were the hearts of everyone present. We spent the evening together, with the members of the small group asking questions and explaining their heart to us. They didn't just want to write a big check and make all of Rocio's problems disappear with money; they were genuinely interested in her emotional and spiritual well-being, and they wanted to get to know her as a person, not just another "project" to throw money at.

When we left that night, we didn't know exactly what they were going to do for Rocio, but we knew for sure that God was answering our prayers.

A few days later, we all gathered at Chick-fil-A. The small group members and representatives from the radio station were all present. It was there that we learned that KLTY had chosen Rocio's story to feature on-air.

The radio show host went on the air with the leader of the small group and Rocio while Maritza and I looked on from the background, not quite sure if what we were seeing was really happening or if it was all just a dream.

The small group leader told Rocio's story to listeners all across DFW. He talked about her struggle, that seemingly random day at Olive Garden, and how a young couple had stepped out in faith to do what they could even though they couldn't do everything they wanted to. He talked about his small group, and how God had led them to help someone who was hurting this holiday season. I noted that he articulated their vision with a high level of love and compassion. And then, he dropped the bomb ...

He announced that they had bought all new furniture and a new TV for her apartment as well as Christmas presents for her boys. And he told her that they were going to take care of her rent for the next six months as well as give her gift cards to Kroger and Target each month for the next six months.

I quickly ran some numbers in my head, and was overwhelmed when I realized that all of this amounted to more than $10,000.

Have you ever been so happy that you wanted to laugh and scream for joy, yet so in awe that you want to cry at the same time? We couldn't believe it was all real, and I don't think Rocio could either. She was in tears, completely stunned by how much God had done for her through His people.

Still on the air, the small group leader turned to us and said, "We want to bless Luke and Maritza too, because of their heart and boldness to step out and ask a stranger if she needed prayer." He handed us a small gift box containing $400 cash and $100 worth of gift cards—to Olive Garden, of course.

Shocked, we just stared at each other, as if to say, "Did that just happen?"

As time went on, Rocio began attending Watermark, and the small group that helped her began meeting with her in her home on Thursday nights for discipleship. She developed such a hunger for the things of God, and we were honored to have her attend our wedding the following summer.

The following year, the small group gave Rocio's family Christmas gifts again—this time without the media fanfare.

The whole experience was amazing, because it turned into something so much bigger than anything we could create on our own. In a moment where we were so focused on our future as a couple, we invited God into our story by getting outside of ourselves and asking our waitress a simple question. He interrupted our day and hijacked our plans, and we couldn't have been happier.

This encounter taught us a lot about the power of simple obedience, and it also impacted the way we viewed generosity. There are countless people out there with real needs and real pain, and they need Christians who will not simply sit by and argue whether or not giving is "biblical"—but instead, open their hearts and their hands.

Maritza and I began to see money as a tool that can make a massive impact for the Kingdom when utilized properly. We realized that our money goes so much further when we use it to help those in need, rather than acquiring more extra stuff that we don't really need. Our hearts were awakened to the reality that God has great things in store for those who choose to live with open hands, rather than tightly clenched fists.

Let's take another look at Malachi 3:10, this time in The Message paraphrase:

> Bring your full tithe to the Temple treasury so there will be ample provisions in my Temple. Test me in this and see if I don't open up heaven itself to you and pour out blessings beyond your wildest dreams. For my part, I will defend you against marauders, protect your wheat fields and vegetable gardens against plunderers.

Sometimes, our lives are marked by moments when God unexpectedly shows up out of nowhere. Other times, we grow through steps of obedience that we take in faith, even if we don't feel God's presence in the moment. Regardless of how God shows up, we can be confident that He is with us, He is for us, and He is faithful to fulfill all that He has promised. And while He doesn't promise us a 100% success rate, He does promise to never leave us, and if you've spent any time with God, you know that no matter what happens, He is enough.

CHAPTER 15

A Businessman, a Prayer, and a Big Surprise

ast forward a few months from when the Christmas miracle took place. It was the summer of 2011, and Maritza and I had just gotten married and were experiencing total newlywed bliss. Our hearts were full, and we were loving every moment as we figured out life together.

In the back of my mind, I remembered how numerous couples had warned us that the first year of marriage is the most difficult, so I kept anticipating the first year struggle to set in. A couple of months passed, and we were still on cloud nine. As the months added up to a year, I realized that the struggle had never arrived.

Sure, we had our share of minor fights. We disagreed about who did the dishes the right way, where my dirty undergarments belonged, and so on, but we didn't experience the difficulty that so many of our friends had warned us about.

Just because you had it rough, doesn't mean we have to, I would say to myself. *Don't project your disappointments and frustrations onto our marriage. It is what you make it!*

You see, we have more control over our circumstances and relationships than we'd like to believe, but we often convince ourselves that we don't so we can avoid embracing the responsibility that this adds.

Maritza and I were learning and growing together. Our hearts were expectant for the future, and we were determined to find God's deeper purpose for our marriage—beyond kids, a minivan, dog, and white picket fence. All of those things are great (yes, even the minivan), but in our hearts, we were hungry for more, we just weren't entirely sure what it was that we were hungry for.

Our experience the year before with Rocio had opened our minds to the possibility that God was teaching us something about money, but we were on the forefront of the journey and didn't have much to go on. We certainly were not ready to start a series of *God's Money Seminars* with *Luke and Maritza International Ministries*, complete with a TV broadcast where we sent out prayer hankies and anointed, gold-plated dollar bills. Still, we felt there was something there.

Summer gave way to fall. Maritza was working at a credit union, held a second part-time job, and was beginning school to work toward her bachelor's degree. I was working full-time doing social media and video editing for a large ministry in Fort Worth. I enjoyed my job for the most part, and we, collectively, made a pretty decent income for a newly married couple in their mid-20's.

Maritza had worked very hard to pay off her car before we got married, and we were determined to avoid car payments for the duration of our lives together. One of our core values was to live below our means so we would have money to spare to be generous and advance the Kingdom, which was over and above our tithe off the top of whatever we made.

There was, however, one small glitch in our plan. I had started using a credit card while finishing ministry school at Heartland, and I still owed roughly $1,100 on it. It felt like a weight over my head, and I felt even more guilty because this decision did not align with our core values and my wife had worked hard to become debt-free before we tied the knot. I knew I couldn't let my credit card balance remain outstanding, so I started working a second job waiting tables at a fancy restaurant in the Southlake Hilton hotel. I had worked there all through ministry school and had built a level of rapport with the managers, so they allowed me to come and go on the schedule as I desired with no pressure to work a certain number of hours each week.

With the holidays approaching, I decided to get busy and crank my hustle knob up a notch. Everyone in DFW goes out to eat around the holidays. Okay, we go out to eat pretty much all the time, but it definitely picks up between Thanksgiving and Christmas. This was easily one of the most lucrative times of the year for the restaurant, especially since we were located inside an upscale hotel in Southlake, one of the wealthiest parts of Tarrant County. My goal of eliminating my debt before Christmas was a pretty realistic one.

I was actually one of the original waitstaff back when the place opened in the summer of 2007. So by this point, I had worked there for the better part of four years. It helped me get through ministry school, supported my church internship, and supplemented my income while I was a missionary associate with Youth Alive. I would occasionally take a month off to travel or skip a few weekends when ministry opportunities came up, but my managers were very lenient with me, because it's actually quite uncommon for servers to stay at one restaurant for that long.

Over the years, I had earned the nickname *Preacher Luke* from my colleagues, who knew that I had attended ministry school and held a variety of positions with a few different ministries. One year, we had a Christmas party at one of the server's homes, and I brought a Bible for the white elephant gift exchange, which of course, solidified the label I willingly embraced.

The restaurant I worked in is a small chain here in the South (mostly in Louisiana). The Southlake Hilton location happened to be the only one in Texas, so we had our fair share of regulars, mostly cajun transplants who ate at Copeland's often before leaving LA for the Lone Star State. We had a cool bar area with some unique drinks, and the whole place had a very classy vibe that attracted many well-off locals. I really enjoyed getting to know the regulars, especially one in particular.

Gavin was a local business owner who would come in once or twice a week and hang out at the bar. That wasn't the area I covered, but I would still stop in and chat with him if I wasn't busy. He was a really nice guy with an inviting smile and great sense of humor. It didn't really matter who was present or where the conversation was headed, Gavin would draw you in and make you feel like he genuinely cared about what was taking place in your life.

He was clean cut and sharply dressed, appropriate for the line of business he worked in. The gleam in his eye and professional air about him quickly put you at ease. He was the type of guy you immediately knew you could trust, and his pepper gray hair made it hard to tell if he was old enough to be my dad or granddad.

One way or another, Gavin caught wind that I was a minister, and he quickly added my nickname to his already extensive vocabulary.

I usually arrived for work at 5:30, right as he was settling in to cap off the day with his usual gin and tonic. "Preacher Luke!", he would exclaim as I came strolling in. We'd typically spend a few minutes catching up before the dinner rush began. I learned about his life, his upbringing, his family, and his business. He talked about how he grew up in one denomination, his wife in another, so they never could really settle on a church to attend together. He deeply respected God and church, but it didn't necessarily come across as a big priority in his present-day life.

Gavin would often tell me that he was proud of me, that he respected the fact that I was so young and eager to pursue a closer relationship with God. He seemed fascinated with my endeavors, and would always ask where I had spoken this week, what I had preached on. He was so genuine, and although we didn't see eye-to-eye on everything, I greatly enjoyed his company. He would ask me about my fiancé, often butchering the pronunciation of her name. After we got married, I shared our wedding pictures and video with him.

One day during my "debt repayment hustle," I found myself frustrated and overwhelmed. Here I was, just a few months in on my marriage, and I already felt like I was getting a bit lazy, a bit less intentional. Like I said, we never had any major struggles, but I found myself caught in a rut where I just didn't feel like trying anymore. I stopped putting as much thought into our date nights even though I wanted to be extravagant and romantic (especially since one of my wife's top Love Languages is "gifts"). I also felt torn, because the weight of my debt weighed heavy on my shoulders, and I was determined to knock it out quickly. But how was I supposed to throw every spare dollar toward paying off my credit card and still get my wife gifts and take her on a nice date every now and then?

I arrived at work thirty minutes early one day, ready to hustle. These thoughts were swirling in my mind as I suited up in my uniform and made my way to the private room we used for breaks and meals, which I found to be empty.

"Help," I quietly whispered to God. "I need Your help! I want to make my wife feel like a princess, but I feel like I can't even begin to do that when I'm so focused on paying off this debt. I know You are for my marriage and You are for me even in my financial foolishness. Please help me. I want to get my edge back; I want to be as romantic as I was when we were engaged. I need Your help."

That was it. I didn't weep, tear my clothes, or engage in a period of intense intercession. All I did was whisper a few sentences to God that expressed the cry of my heart.

With a sigh, I made my way to the front of the house for my shift and the night progressed like all the others.

The next day was Friday, one of our busiest nights of the week. Around 6:30, the dinner rush was well underway. As they say in the industry, I was "in the weeds"—meaning I had more going on than I could keep up with. Flustered, I did the best I could to keep my head above water. At one point, I was in the back pouring some ice waters for a table, when Laura (one of the bartenders) came by and grabbed my arm.

"Hey Luke, Gavin's here and wants to see you for a sec."

She must have noticed how busy I was (perhaps my sweaty red face gave it away?), because she quickly added, "Just, uh, whenever you get a minute."

"Alright," I replied. "Tell him it's gonna be a few, but I'll be there soon."

I resumed my work, and eventually, arrived at a more manageable pace. That was when it hit me. *Gavin! Oh, no. It's been nearly an hour since Laura told me he wanted to see me.*

I quickly made my way to the bar. Scanning the room, he was nowhere to be found.

"Hey Laura, is Gavin still here?"

"No, he left awhile ago. But he gave me this for you."

She handed me a crumpled napkin that I could tell had something wrapped inside.

As I always tried to stay professional in front of customers, I shoved it into my pocket and made my way to the break room.

Scrawled in barely legible writing, amidst drink stains, was a note from Gavin.

"Preacher!" it read. "I'm so proud of you. Treat your wife to something nice—on me."

As I unfolded the napkin further, my jaw dropped.

Enclosed was a $100 bill.

I sat there, stunned. It was a good thing I wasn't still swamped, because I really needed a minute this time. Tears welled up in my eyes as I remembered the quick prayer I had lifted up the day before.

Wow, God. You were really listening. Thank you!

It's one thing to know that God answers prayers, and another thing to actually experience it—especially when God answers those off-the-cuff, moment-of-desperation prayers that often slip your mind the moment they've left your lips.

Looking back, $100 doesn't necessarily seem like a ton of money. But to me, in that moment, it felt like I had just won the lottery. It was significant, because I had just prayed for financial help, for God to equip me to be the husband I wanted to be to Maritza. And then, the very next day, an acquaintance hands me money intended for that very purpose, completely oblivious to my inner frustration. This meant so much more than a random check in the mail or a $100 bonus; it was a picture of God coming through in the way He does best—extravagantly, catching us off guard.

I was ecstatic, but managed to keep the exchange a secret from my wife. I got in touch with Gavin, and let him know how grateful I was, then went out and bought Maritza some jewelry and accessories I knew she would love. After hiding the gift bag in my car, I told her I wanted to take her out on a date, but that it would probably be someplace quick and cheap, since we're focused on paying off our debt.

Earlier in our marriage, we had mutually determined our favorite spot to get sushi in the city. It was a rare treat, since it was priced quite a bit higher than other sushi places in the area.

That night, I began driving toward that part of town, with Maritza trying to figure out where we would be eating the whole way. As I pulled into the parking lot of the sushi place, she had a look of disbelief on her face.

"But, I thought ..."

"Let me tell you a story," I said with a smile.

I told her the entire story as we sat in my car. I then pulled out the gift bag, she cried a bit, and we headed inside. As we shared a wonderful meal together, we were so in awe of how God had come through for us in such an intimate, personal way. Gavin probably didn't realize it, but he was being used by God to blow our minds. The most amazing part was it wasn't even something we needed. God cares about our unspoken, secret desires. He doesn't just want to give us the things we need to barely survive, but the little things that make our hearts come alive as well. What began as a simple prayer in the back room of a restaurant turned into a small miracle that served as the second milestone on our journey of trusting God with our finances.

What's your secret desire that feels like it's not worth praying about?

I think God wants to talk to you about that very thing, no matter how ridiculous it may seem.

CHAPTER 16

You and Your Sacrifice; How Cute!

W hat started as some small lessons of generosity had begun to snowball in our marriage, and we were loving it. These occurrences had led us to a place of deeper expectation that God had big plans for our money, as if we were tasting appetizers that were only teasers of the meal that was to come or watching trailers for a new movie that we were really looking forward to.

Our experiences so far had been enlightening and eye opening, but nothing felt like it had really altered our own life courses or contributed to moving us toward our destinies. We felt we had made an impact in our friend Rocio's life, but hadn't seen any major shifts in our own lives. Not that we were necessarily expecting that or desperately looking for it, it just hadn't happened, and after awhile, it had begun to feel as though our lives were stagnant.

In a bizarre collision of paths that some would call coincidence, the weekend that God surprised us with the sushi money through Gavin was the same window of time that a new sermon series was beginning at our church. The topic of this series was tithing, financial blessings and curses, and putting God first in your life.

The six week series opened our eyes to concepts that we felt God was already teaching us, providing a biblical foundation for what we had already been thinking and feeling. This only confirmed that God truly desired to instill these concepts regarding generosity deep into our hearts in order to be a blessing to others. However, it also caused us to look long and hard at how we viewed tithing as a married couple. We had both been raised to tithe, and carried a similar view on tithing throughout our adult lives and into our marriage.

But we had never really asked ourselves why we did this or been challenged to grow in the area. We took the teachings of this sermon series to heart, examining our bank accounts, giving statements, and the Scriptures to discover what we *really* believed. Finally, we looked ourselves in the mirror and asked ourselves *why* we did the things we did. This was a critical step in obtaining a clear view of what was taking place below the surface and what needed to change in our hearts in terms of how we approached giving and generosity. Looking at any area of your life and admitting there is room for growth isn't always fun, but it's necessary.

Compared to other young, married couples in our age group, we were doing fine financially. I had paid off the last of my credit card debt, we were paying all our bills, and even saving for a house. We tithed the first 10% of our income to our church, sponsored a child in Haiti, and had given generously on top of the tithe. We lived within our means and had money to spare, which we immediately rolled over into our savings account. Sure, we wasted a little money on frivolous things, but overall we had established and stuck to a healthy budget.

By the end of the series, the pastor challenged everyone to ask the Holy Spirit what He was saying to them about this topic; to go home, pray as a family, and seek God for what needed to be rearranged in order to place Him at the helm of their finances.

Maritza and I took the challenge. We sought God, and felt Him challenge us to do something we'd never done or even seemed modeled. By this time, it was November of 2011, and we were both still working multiple jobs, so this made us a bit nervous. However, we decided to follow God's leading and take two action steps—one big and the other a bit smaller.

The first step involved a missionary friend we knew from ministry school. She was taking big risks and living by faith in order to do a great work for the Kingdom, and we felt the Lord putting it on our hearts to give her a large financial gift—large for us at the time, at least.

The second step was a prompting to sow our entire first paychecks of the new year (2012) into an offering. This was absolutely terrifying. We weren't rich, we had just finished paying off my credit card balance, and we were saving every spare cent to apply toward the down payment on our first home. We essentially lived paycheck to paycheck, and certainly didn't have any extra money lying around to throw in the offering plate. If we were to do this, we knew it would be a stretch and require a lot of sacrifice, but it's what we felt God leading us to do. We could feel the wind of heaven at our backs and knew God had something great in store for us on the other side of this extravagant risk.

I feel the need to pause here for a bit of clarification. Hear my heart in this—I don't tell you this story because I think you need to be like us and give an entire first paycheck or empty your savings in order to be blessed. I'm not some weird televangelist promising that if you send in the only money you have to buy groceries, God will give it all back to you and then some. This isn't the heart of God; it's manipulation. And for us, it was less about the actual giving of money and more about what God was doing in our hearts. He was teaching us to be generous, to take risks, and to trust Him. This is the way that He did it, but His process in your life may look totally different.

I think the reason why God led us to take these big steps of faith was because we needed to be pushed out of our comfort zones. We had been coasting on the beliefs we had held since childhood. We had never really taken any risks or done anything full of crazy—almost stupid—faith, but God was inviting us to a deeper relationship with Him.

Once we decided to take these risks, we immediately began to prepare. We budgeted a bit tighter and were ready to give up our first paychecks come January. It wasn't easy over the holidays, but we were determined to make it work and convinced that we must be obedient to God no matter the cost.

Shortly before Christmas, we agreed on a number to give to our missionary friend, but had not written the check yet. We then found out that she would be passing through town briefly, and we agreed to host her for a night at our apartment. It was short notice, but we figured it would be a good opportunity to go ahead and write her a check at the same time, so she could use it for her holidays or whatever else she would need upon returning to the mission field.

A few days before she was scheduled to arrive, we received a random, totally unrelated check in the mail—for exactly *double* the amount we had planned to give to our missionary friend. The source was unexpected, the timing was random, and the amount made us laugh in joy and a bit of disbelief. We were stunned. Even though this was the smaller of the two action steps, it was still a stretch for us, but God had provided in a big way before we had even taken the step! Though we were caught off guard, we had almost come to expect these types of miracles from the Lord.

Why is this, you may ask?

You see, we understand this spiritual principal called "sowing and reaping." The world may call this "karma," but the Jesus version is far better—in this instance, we reaped before we had sowed! We were committed to do so, but the money had not yet left our hands. We had purchased the seeds and now, a harvest was waiting for us, even though we had not gotten around to planting them yet. I had never heard anyone teach about God's laws of multiplication in this manner, and I'm not sure if this is how He normally does things, but this was our experience. I think sometimes God switches up the game to show us how good He truly is and prevent us from turning things into rigid, religious formulas—rather than faith-filled responses to who God is and what He wants to do in our lives.

I might have been tempted to chalk this up to a random, isolated incident, until I saw what happened next.

● ● ●

If you've used Facebook for any length of time, you've probably seen an annoying tactic used by tabloids and fake news sites called "clickbait." This poor writing technique is used to get the curious and/or gullible to click on articles and videos. Usually, there's nothing malicious behind the articles, like a virus or anything, it's simply a classless and cheesy style that some marketers use in hopes to get more clicks that translate into more ad sales.

This Man Found a Puppy Stranded in a Roadside Ditch—What Happens Next Will Shock You!

This is a prime example of clickbait.

I cannot stand this as a style of writing for headlines, as I feel it is lazy and immature. However, if I were to write about this next milestone in my story in this style, it would sound something like this: *One Couple Feels Prompted to Give Away Their Entire First Paychecks of 2012 — You Won't Believe What Happens Next!*

Christmas had come and gone, and we were ready for "the big give." My first paycheck was scheduled to direct-deposit to our account on January 6th, and Maritza's would hit a day or two later.

On December 31, we were attending a prophetic prayer service in a local church plant that I seen promoted on Facebook. As a couple, Maritza and I are committed to honor God with our entire lives, not just our finances. We looked forward to ringing in the new year with prayer and prophetic ministry, while many others our age were attending parties and celebrations across the metroplex. It was an incredible night, and there were some words spoken over us that we will treasure for the rest of our lives.

By Monday morning, January 2, we were back to work as usual. I didn't hate my job, but I didn't love it, either. I knew it wasn't a long-term gig and I was simply there for a season, so though I was caught in the frustrating place between loving and hating it, I wasn't actively looking for a new opportunity. I had only logged nine months on the payroll, and was planning on putting in more time before moving on.

The next day, I received a call from a number I didn't recognize. I was about to take my lunch break for the day, so I stepped out of my cube and took the call. As it turned out, it was an old acquaintance I'd stayed connected with via social media. We had gone to church together for a season, and I knew his son from the youth group. He ran his own business, and I was intrigued to see a business leader who was committed to following Jesus and operating with a high level of integrity.

We briefly exchanged pleasantries before cutting to the chase.

"Are you still doing graphic design and social media stuff?" he asked. "I remember that you were involved in that before, and the person who was running the creative department for our business left a few days ago. I'm looking to hire a replacement; would you be interested in talking about possibly coming to work for me?"

I stammered a bit, trying not to sound too excited about this possibility. "Um, yes sir, I'd, uh, be open to discussing that with you."

"Okay, great!" he replied. "How about you and the wife come over this Friday, so we can get to talking and see if it will be a good fit. Sound good?"

"Yes, sir! Just let me know when and where, and we'll be there."

The call ended, and I sat in silence for a moment, completely stunned. *Wow,* I thought to myself. *I did not see that coming!* I returned to my desk, attempting to act normal. All the while, below the surface, my heart was full of wonder, expectancy, and possibility.

That evening, Maritza and I talked about this discussion. She seemed excited about the opportunity, and was open to the idea of making a change.

When Friday rolled around, we all had a wonderful time connecting. The man who had called me provided insight into his business, the role he needed to fill, and more details as to what it would entail. He asked how much I was currently making and what I expected my schedule to look like, but aside from that, the evening was very relationally-driven. It didn't feel like a typical job interview, which I appreciated, because I was ready for something different even though I was nervous because I wasn't planning on taking action and actually choosing something different at this point in my career and marriage.

At one point, he threw out a number that they were considering as a starting salary for the position. I tried to hide my disbelief. It was a substantial leap from what I was currently making—to do the same thing in a better environment. I was anticipating that this would be a lateral move in terms of income, but I was entertaining the idea because the idea of going from a large, ministry/corporate environment to a small team that behaved more like a startup was appealing to me.

This couple seemed so genuine and deep; they showed their personalities and hearts beyond the "surface-level" that you usually get from businesspeople, yet they were professional at the same time. They were the kind of people you just wanted to be around, even if you had only had a brief interaction with them.

I left them with my resume, references, and work portfolio—which almost seemed pointless, because I felt as though they cared less about that and more about me as a person. They told me they would fast and pray over the next few days, as they took hiring very seriously. "We try to build family—not just workers or employees. So we are very deliberate in the process. You can expect to hear a 'yes' or 'no' from us very soon, as we don't want to waste your time. We will be in touch by Monday at the latest."

As we were driving home, Maritza and I were blown away that the opportunity had even presented itself. This couple was the real deal, and the pros of the situation were abundant, with little to no cons in sight when I took my current job into consideration. We tried not to get too excited, as it was not yet locked in and the salary seemed almost too good to be true.

The next few days were an emotional rollercoaster of dreaming and waiting. It was only a weekend, but my level of anticipation was building as I eagerly awaited Monday; I wanted to know one way or another so I could either celebrate a new season or fully embrace my current one.

We were sitting on the couch in our apartment on Sunday afternoon watching *House Hunters* on HGTV (no shame) when my phone rang. When I saw the name on the caller ID, I quickly lowered the volume and stepped into the other room.

"Luke, if you're ready, we'd love to have you on board. We'll pay you ___ per year, and you can start as soon as you'd like—the sooner the better."

We quickly worked through the details, and I was holding back tears as I hung up the phone. This opportunity seemed so random, but I knew God had been at work behind the scenes and had orchestrated all the details—all the way down to asking us to trust Him by giving up our entire paychecks, right before he blew our minds with something better than what we knew to ask for.

I walked back into the living room, where my wife was still sitting on the couch, and told her the news. We cried together, tears of joy. Suddenly, something clicked in my head, seemingly out of the blue.

"Baby!" My tone shifted from joyous to shock.

"What, Luke?!"

"Do you realize ..." I trailed off for a moment, as I double-checked the math in my head. "Wow," I said aloud.

Let's pause for a moment. Like with the missionary, we had not yet given the "first fruits" offering of our entire paychecks when this milestone took place; we had only made the decision and committed to doing so. We were once again seeing God open a door in response to the decision we made in our hearts, before the actual action took place.

The reason why I said "wow" is because when I added up the numbers in my head that afternoon, it was too coincidental to pass up. (By now, you likely know that I don't really believe in 'coincidence.') My salary with this new job was further confirmation that God's fingerprints were all over this whole thing. When I broke it down monthly, I realized I would be making the same amount of money as my previous job, plus the exact amount of money (within two dollars) from the paychecks we gave away, in addition each month.

In case that figure doesn't immediately make sense, imagine that I made $1,000/month at my previous job, and gave away mine and my wife's paychecks from the beginning of the year, for a total amount of $1,500. My new job would have me making $2,500/month—the same as before, plus the amount we gave away. We didn't just get that money back one time, but every single month. (For the record, these are not the actual numbers.)

Isn't God good?! This completely blew our minds. It was as if God was saying, "Oh, you guys are so cute! You've worked so hard and have been so sacrificial in your obedience. I know you were nervous. I know you wondered if it would be worth it in the end. Well, watch this! See how easily I can give back everything you've sacrificed—and then some?!"

We were awestruck, and still are, anytime we think about this. It forever "sealed the deal" in our hearts that we could never out-give God. For us, this is the only way to live—generously. Obedience and generosity combined are a powerful addition to your arsenal of tools for your spiritual journey, so you can go forward once you're in, without turning back.

From time to time, I'll have a conversation with a fellow believer who is struggling a great deal with money. They find themselves stuck in a rut where they can never seem to get ahead, no matter how hard they hustle.

When I find myself in these conversations, I try to be a good listener, smile, nod, and offer quasi-helpful solutions, but I really want to look them square in the eyes and ask them how much of a giver they've been lately. Perhaps one day I'll move beyond my fears and actually do this, but for now, it's remained in the back of my mind.

My experience is that God does not bless hands that are tightly clenched shut, no matter how fast we run or how hard we hustle. The harder I hold on to my money, refusing to be generous because "I barely have enough myself," the worse off my financial state becomes. However, the more I surrender to God and honor Him by being a good steward and giving generously (it's about the percentage, not the amount), the more joy, peace, success, and abundance I experience in my life.

This has been my first-hand experience, but I certainly don't have all the answers. For example, there are plenty of millionaires all over the world that are incredibly wealthy and successful, yet have never honored God with a dime. I don't get that, but I would much rather have my treasure later than have it now and leave God out of the process.

Generosity is much more of a heart issue than a bank account issue. When you're not putting God first in your life, you're bound to struggle. We simply cannot make life work on our own, but the good news is that we were never intended to, and we don't have to. We have a Helper, and He will help us get it right.

I'm not saying you have to empty out your bank account and run to your local homeless shelter, dumping a pile of money on a table as a heroic act of sacrifice. There is no magical formula for guaranteed financial results, regardless of how many preachers have told you that the windows of heaven will unlock if you just sow a $39 seed, and I don't stand to make a dime from you opening your heart to the idea of becoming a more generous person.

Start *where* you can, as *soon* as you can, and see what God does! Unclench your fists and let God in—when He is first place in your heart, your hands will follow suit. Don't just take my word for it; put your trust in a limitless God who cares about the smallest and most mundane details of your life.

To this day, Maritza and I continue to live a generous lifestyle, bless others, and financially support our local church through tithing at least ten percent of our income. I'm convinced that one day, we'll look back on these chapters and see that they were only the beginning, even though at the time, they seemed like huge risks.

Editor's Note: I have personally known Luke for eight years and would meet him for lunch every other month or so while these things were taking place in his life. At the time that he and Maritza were taking these risks and blessing others financially, they were very quiet and low-key about how God was enabling them to make a difference in the lives of others. They share these stories, not to stand on the street corner and showcase their righteous acts like the Pharisees of Jesus' day, but to encourage others to live a satisfying and fulfilling life of following Jesus—no matter what the cost.

CHAPTER 17

Crafting Your Story

I t was the fall of 2008. I was a year in with my ministry school education and was growing in my relationship with God as I became more and more passionate about seeing people come to know Him.

I was driving through north Fort Worth one evening, toward my favorite Starbucks, when I noticed a woman making her way down the street in a wheelchair. The thought to stop and pray for her crossed my mind, and I briefly slowed my truck.

At the time, I was a part of a small group led by a pastor from my church who was very intentional about encouraging us to take our faith public. He would often quote Bill Johnson, a pastor in California, saying, "If you are a believer, the Holy Spirit is inside of you—and He wants out!"

In context, this simply means to see the world around you through spiritual lenses and look for opportunities to minister to those you come in contact with on a daily basis. This isn't necessarily a charismatic thing, but something that all believers are invited to tap into to make a difference in the world around them.

All of these thoughts raced through my head as I cruised past the lady in the wheelchair. Finally, I gave in and tapped the brakes. I turned around and drove the two blocks back to where she was, my mind churning as I tried to figure out what I would say to this lady so she wouldn't think I was completely crazy.

I thought back to the time in the Mennonite church in Pennsylvania when the pastor prayed for my back and the Lord met me in a very tangible way. I had experienced His healing power in my own life and in the lives of others as well. It's not something I fully understand, but I have read about it throughout the Scriptures, and have my own first-hand experience. It's one thing to have a theology for something and another to actually have a real-life experience to back it up—especially when it's your own experience and not just the experience of another.

I pulled to a stop a few dozen yards in front of the lady in the wheelchair, turned my hazard lights on, and exited my truck. I was nervous, but smiled as I slowly approached the woman on the side of the road. I could almost picture the Lord healing her in my mind—but, more importantly, I was being obedient to His prompting to step out and be a witness to my faith.

"Excuse me, ma'am," I said as our paths crossed. I had only lived in Texas for a few years, but had quickly adopted the Southern hospitality and added terms like *sir, ma'am,* and *y'all* to my vocabulary.

She stopped for a moment and looked up at me, fairly oblivious to my approach until I spoke. I was certain she would have heard my heart pounding in my chest before I stepped out of my truck, but at this point, my faith was rising and building as I began to imagine what God could do.

I told her I was a Christian, and briefly shared a thirty-second version of my back healing story—how I had suffered from physical pain when I was younger, but God touched my back and a supernatural miracle occurred.

"I noticed you here, and I believe God can touch your back. I think He's in a really good mood today (a line I stole from Pastor Bill Johnson); may I pray for you?"

This is it! I thought to myself. *This is the big moment!* I quickly glanced around, wondering where the Fox4 and NBC5 vans would park in order to broadcast the supernatural testimony to God's power that was about to take place.

The woman smiled and sweetly shook her head. "No thanks!" she replied. "I'm good. But have a great evening!" With that, she put her hands back on her wheels and was on her way.

I don't think I said anything in reply. I was speechless. Emotions of confusion, offense, embarrassment, and relief welled up inside of me, blending together into something I tried to push down as I walked back to my truck. Climbing into the driver's seat, I let out a sigh as I started the engine and drove off.

This event took some time for me to process. I didn't really share the story, as I was frustrated that this faith-filled moment had fallen flat. Since then, I've prayed for others who needed healing and have seen God touch their lives, which makes me wonder what would have happened to the lady in the wheelchair if she had just been willing to let a stranger say a simple prayer on her behalf. Now that several years have passed, however, I realize I need to let go of thoughts like this, because I did my part and was obedient to God's leading in the moment. I was faithful to do what I could do in telling my story of what God had done in my own life, but the rest was between her and God. I couldn't force her to put her plans for the evening on hold to receive prayer, and I wasn't going to follow her around all night praying under my breath, as that would probably freak her out.

You are not responsible for the outcome when you share Christ or tell your story. All you are responsible for is crafting your story and telling it well.

● ● ●

Crafting Your Story

Now that you've learned about the power of story and [hopefully] drawn inspiration from my story, let's take some time to put it all together as you begin the process of crafting your own story. This book is intended to be so much more than a nice collection of stories about the life of a dorky white guy in Texas; I want you to walk away feeling like you can take the stories that lie within you and articulate them to the world.

You may already have several stories of God moving in your life in ways both large and small, and that's great. For each story you can think of, I'd like to give you a few practical steps you can take and immediately live out in the "real world." My goal is that these stories would move beyond the archives of your mind and be released to the world, to be captured by the hearts of those you come into contact with.

First, grab a blank journal. Get ready to take a trip down memory lane. As stories come to mind, you need to have a place to record them. (You can also use a computer if that's helpful, although I have found it's distracting for this step.)

Next, remember. Put on some worship jams or sit in silence. Go people watch at the airport. Take a shower. Talk to your parents or spouse. Lie in bed and stare at the ceiling. Just do something that will get your memory going and recall to the surface the moments when God has moved in your life. This process may take time. In order to articulate Rocio's story, I had several conversations with my wife to get all the details squared away.

Jot down brief, bullet points of the story. Just capture the big idea here, with perhaps, a few details. Some of you may choose to write out the whole thing, but this is counterproductive for most. If you begin with bullet points, you'll likely find it gets your creative juices flowing, which will enhance the quality of your writing when you record the finer details.

Personally, I can recall a complete story from bullet points of the key moments. This skeleton enables me to write entire essays, or prepare the story for a talk if I'm communicating it in that manner.

Here is a quick and easy template to build a skeleton framework:

- Where you were at in life?
- What happened to you?
- What changed in your life?
- What does your life look like now?

It's important to remember to focus more on what God did rather than the slump you were in or the weight of any oppression you felt. I've heard far too many stories where the person spends three minutes talking about how miserable they were, how lost they were, how hard life was, how wild and crazy their sin was—and then follow it up with a God spotlight that only lasts thirty seconds. Why not give the glory to the One who rescued you instead? My recommendation is to spend 25 percent of the story talking about the "before Christ" portion of your story and 75 percent telling your "after Christ" story.

Tell yourself the story. I'm sure I occasionally look like a crazy person during my morning commute when I decide to practice sharing a story with the dashboard. This gives me a solid 45 minutes to practice telling my story well and identify ways I can make it better. I sometimes use the voice memo feature on my iPhone to play back my story to ensure it is engaging and worth listening to. I ask myself, "If I were a stranger hearing this story, would I pay attention?"

Craft different versions of the story. Sometimes you'll only have a 30-second window with a stranger, while other times you'll end up stuck talking to your wife's sister's boyfriend at a party for 45 minutes.

I'm not saying you need two versions with totally different details to appeal to different people groups, but you do need to be prepared for various circumstances. Don't leave this to chance. Find a way to time yourself (your smartphone could come in handy here) and become comfortable telling your story within various timeframes.

30-Second Version

Hustling entrepreneurs and tech startup CEO's spend *hours* crafting a 30-second business pitch, just in case they meet an investor in an elevator or at the airport. Are you just as prepared to "pitch God" to someone who needs to hear the Story in a pinch?

2-Minute Version

This will carry the same urgency and tone as the 30 second pitch, but you can draw out a few more details and give a stronger message overall. This is the "trailer" to the movie of the gospel...if someone watched the 2 minutes, would they want to see the whole thing?

10-Minute Version

This is your moment to really craft your story in the same way that a hipster woodworker crafts an artisan table out of reclaimed wood pallets and locally-sourced beaver tails. Get all the details in there, fully display the brokenness of the "before" situation, and deeply emphasize the radical change brought on by the goodness of God. I love how Bill Johnson says, "God is better than we think." Does your story convince others that God is worth paying attention to?

Update the software. Has it been awhile since you've told your story? Or have you lost your original passion that you once had when the stories were fresh in your heart? You may need to plug into the "App Developer" and ask Him to give you a refresh.

This process shouldn't take you more than a couple of days for each story; don't get super hung up on perfectionism. If your story is 80 percent complete and shared with the world, it's still better than 100 percent perfect and stuck in the land of missed opportunity. Once you're generally confident in your ability to tell your story, it's time to begin sharing it.

● ● ●

Sharing Your Story

There's a ton of great resources on evangelism and plenty of methods for sharing your faith (some of which are outdated). I'd like to outline a couple of methods that I find helpful when initiating a conversation. These would have helped me greatly with the wheelchair lady, but I had not heard of them at the time. (Next time you run into a wheelchair lady, you won't have that excuse.)

SALT

Several years ago, I became connected with a global church planting and missions movement called Every Nation. This organization formed in 1994 when Rice Broocks, Phil Bonasso, and Steve Murrell aligned their churches and ministries to pursue the mission of church planting, campus ministry, and global missions.

At the time, Rice was a student evangelist in Nashville, Tennessee, Phil was a church planter in Southern California, and Steve was a missionary in the Philippines. In February of 1994, Rice and Phil traveled to Asia to explore church planting opportunities in Singapore and Malaysia. On the way home, they stopped in Manila to visit Steve and discuss the possibility of collaborating on the new church plant. As they sat in Steve's living room, they began to reflect on their common vision to plant churches and campus ministries in every nation of the earth. That night, they committed to pursue this mission together.

Since that day in 1994, Every Nation has planted churches and campus ministries in sixty nations that span six continents. Last year, I was blessed with the opportunity to sit down with Dr. Rice Broocks for a few days and hear his heart for evangelism, missions, and the local church. It was through Every Nation that I discovered the SALT method of evangelism, and it fits perfectly here as a tool to aid you in crafting and sharing your story:

Start a Conversation

Engaging someone in conversation is easy to do—most of the time. It begins with looking up from your phone, smiling, and saying "Hi!"

Ask Questions

Show the other person that you're interested in getting to know them and connecting with them on a personal level.

Listen to the Other Person

Every person has a story to tell, and most people just want someone to listen to them. Take some time to listen to their story before you tell your own.

Tell the Story

When it's your turn to speak, you can transition into sharing the story of how Jesus impacted and changed your life.

You are the salt of the earth. But if the salt loses its saltiness, how can it be made salty again? It is no longer good for anything, except to be thrown out and trampled by men. You are the light of the world. A city on a hill cannot be hidden. Neither do people light a lamp and put it under a bowl. Instead they put it on its stand, and it gives light to everyone in the house. In the same way, let your light shine before men, that they may see your good deeds and praise your Father in heaven. -Matthew 5:13-16, NIV.

A huge key here is the actual Gospel Story. I'm making an assumption that you are already a Christian, and if that is true, you know this to be true. However, in this next paragraph, you will find a structured version of the Gospel that tells much of the Story and is easy to memorize. This is another great resource I picked up from Dr. Rice Broocks and Every Nation. Learn it, memorize it, and share it!

The Gospel is the good news that God became man in Jesus Christ. He lived the life we should have lived and died the death we should have died, in our place. Three days later He rose from the dead, proving that He is the Son of God and offering the gift of salvation and forgiveness of sins for all who repent and believe.

Another great resource is the FORM method, which is similar to SALT:

Family
- Where are you from?
- Where did you go to high school/college?
- How many kids do you have? What are their names and ages?
- Are you married? What is your spouse's name?

Occupation
- What kind of work do you do?
- What do you like about your job?
- What do you like least about your job?
- How long have you been working there?
- How did you get started in that field?

Recreation
- What kind of things do you do for fun?
- What type of vacation do you enjoy?
- What are some of your favorite places in the world?

- What do you do to relieve stress?
- What is the most exciting thing you've ever done?

Message
- This is your opportunity to share!

Once you have built rapport with someone, the message portion is really just a transition toward unpacking your own story.

I learned this in the business world as a tool to help me refine my relational skills and ability to connect with people. While some use this method to drive sales, I've found it to be applicable in many other arenas, including ministry.

In a marketing context, the end of the FORM method gives you an opportunity to connect the person to your product or service.

In the quest to tell the story well, FORM is a great way to connect with strangers and open the door to an opportunity to share your story.

Regardless of your angle, the FORM method helps you establish trust, which will increase the odds that they'll actually listen to what you have to say. As with sales, they may not accept your message. They may respond in a similar manner to the wheelchair lady. You never want to make these methods something you use to force something on anyone; they are simply helpful tools to show people that you care about them and to communicate your message—in this instance, your story of the work of God in your life.

In order for FORM to be most effective, the key is *listening*. If you speed through the first three steps just to get to your message, without taking the time to actually listen, you're not going to make the other person listen to what you have to say; in fact, it may actually turn them off from what you have to say! The secret to winning others over is becoming an active listener.

What is an "active listener?" It's when you ask questions and engage in listening to the answer. Instead of using a question to impose your will and story upon someone, you first take a moment to understand what the other person is sharing, and you build your next question on their response so they know you are listening and feel that you value what they have to say. If you want someone to pay attention to your story, the first step is to pay attention to their story.

You should also know that firing off questions without sharing a piece of your own story can feel like an interrogation. You want to first place the focus on the other person's story, but then seek to find a balance between doing all the talking and all the listening—which is where the real, natural flow of conversation takes place.

Have fun with it, and I encourage to experiment by telling your stories to anyone who will listen. This is just the beginning!

CHAPTER 18

Dan Berlin & Co.

C hances are, you've never heard of Dan Berlin.

At one point, he was a normal guy from Fort Collins, Colorado. However, in his mid-30's, a disease called one-rod retinal dystrophy slowly began to wreck havoc on his eyes. His vision began to slowly erode, eventually leaving him completely blind, out of shape, and depressed.

This was a life-altering event, but Dan didn't let it keep him down. On July 4, 2009, he began to run, targeting a half marathon for the fall—not an easy feat when you're blind and live at a high altitude.

When the event neared, Dan felt that his lack of sight might make him a hazard for other runners, so he requested that the race director pair him with another runner. Together, he and his guide finished the half marathon in two hours and ten minutes, which is a great time given the circumstances. [9]

Dan was immediately hooked. He and his guide paired up again to run a full marathon—the 2011 New York City Marathon—but he did not stop there. He went on to run the 2012 Colorado Marathon and 2013 Toughman Half Ironman in New York. And with a little help from his friends, Dan made history at 9:20 on the morning of Wednesday, October 8, 2014.

This was the moment he and four teammates completed the Rim to Rim to Rim, a 46-mile bucket list run for ultra-runners. By this time, Dan was in his mid-40's and was the first blind athlete to complete the grueling run from the South Rim of the Grand Canyon to the North Rim, and back again. This course, which features 29,000 feet of elevation gain, took the team 28 hours to complete.

"I feel great," Dan said after the run.[10] "There were some wonderful moments and there were definitely dark moments. You just don't know what your body is going to do."

I'm not sure how they did it. Did they sleep? Did they run straight through the night? This would be tough enough feat for those who are *not* blind!

As journalist Stephen Meyers artfully explained in the Coloradoan: "Dan Berlin's message is clear: his blindness is an inconvenience, not a disability. His blindness doesn't have to be limiting. His blindness won't keep him from running."

"It (blindness) doesn't have to be limiting," Dan said. It can be an expanding situation to really enjoy doing some great things. A lot of wonderful things have come about because of this this (my blindness)."

What a remarkable story! Like with most great stories, Dan will tell you he didn't pull it off on his own. "Achieving this is an amazing accomplishment for all five of us. This run wouldn't have quite the same meaning without a team to depend on each other."

The Coloradoan mentioned that Dan was guided by Charles Scott (who had previously guided him through his marathons), Alison Berna, Brad Graff, and the final individual was left unnamed. The team used a combination of voice commands, a rigid tether, and trekking poles to help Dan navigate the difficult terrain of the Grand Canyon, a route that often led them past hundred-foot drop-offs on one side.

"He called me asking if I would guide him." Charles said. "I had a lot of self-doubt. ... He just told me, 'Don't worry about it. I'll show you how.' There is something powerful about helping another person. Running Rim to Rim to Rim you're going through various levels of discomfort. When you're taking turns running (for yourself) and then guiding, it takes you out of your self-pity mode that you fall into when you're hurting."

This was illustrated in the final mile up the 6,000-foot climb to the ridge of the North Rim. At this point, Dan had hit a rough patch, but Alison was at a high note. She was full of energy and enthusiasm, going as far as to do handstands near the summit while encouraging Dan, who was hurting both physically and emotionally. He was cold, wrapped in two space blankets, wondering if he would make it to the top, let along back across the canyon; this was only the halfway point! Dan's darkest moment was one of Alison's brightest, but rather than celebrating alone, she helped encourage her friend and gave him an extra push when he needed it most.

"I had never guided a blind athlete before. This was one of my personal fears in doing this. Would I be the right person to guide someone?" Alison said. "I was so high (in that moment). I overcame my fears. I knew then he trusted me. We really came into a rhythm together after that."

Alison told the Coloradoan that the team's fundraising efforts didn't end after the Rim to Rim to Rim run. The team filmed the entire journey on GoPro cameras in hopes of releasing a documentary. Their ongoing campaign raised more than $7,500 for Denver's Blind Institute of Technology and the Foundation Fighting Blindness.

"Think about how devastating it is to lose your sight," Charles said. "I'm sure I would go out and be in despair. Dan's in this situation; it's not fair and it sucks. It can be devastating. Instead, he focuses on what he can do and not what he can't do. It is extremely powerful and inspiring. I hope people see the power that we all have in our own minds to make the most out of our lives and not to be afraid—to know that we can grow and actually live out full lives. Dan inspires me every day."

I could talk about Dan's positive attitude and resilient spirit all day, but instead, I'd like to zero in on some of the other people who played a role in his epic moment: Charles and Alison.

Did you happen to catch what they said about the experience?

This was one of my personal fears in doing this.

Would I be the right person to guide someone?

There is something powerful about helping another person.

When you're taking turns running (for yourself) and then guiding, it takes you out of your self-pity mode that you fall into when you're hurting.

There's something to be said for helping others, and it has a way of giving our own lives a sense of meaning and purpose. When we remove the blinders that cause us to narrow our focus to our own lives, we set ourselves up for some pretty extraordinary things.

CHAPTER 19

Stones of Remembrance

When I first began writing this book three years ago, the working title was *Landmark* and it was about establishing one's personal history with God.

In the book of Joshua, the people of God are on a journey to take hold of the land God had promised them. They had just come out of slavery in Egypt, and their final step was a hazardous journey across the Jordan River, which was in flood stage at the time. As soon as the priests who were carrying the ark of the covenant (which represented God's presence) touched the water's edge with their feet, the river immediately stopped flowing and everyone crossed over to the other side on dry land (Joshua 3:15-17).

Once everyone was across, God spoke to Joshua and told him to have twelve men go back into the river bed and each pick up one large rock. They then carried the rocks to the bank of the river on the side of the promised land and arranged them in a pile as a memorial to the miracle that had just taken place there.

In the future, when your children ask you, "What do these stones mean?" tell them that the flow of the Jordan was cut off before the ark of the covenant of the Lord. When it crossed the Jordan, the waters of the Jordan were cut off. These stones are to be a memorial to the people of Israel forever. -Joshua 4:6b-7, NIV

This memorial wasn't just any memorial, it would serve as a sign to the generations to come of the faithfulness of God. The parting of the Jordan was no small miracle. It often takes a back seat to the parting of the Red Sea, which has had more movies made about it, but imagine for a moment a rushing river at flood stage ceasing to flow while more than 40,000 people crossed the riverbed without getting their feet wet or muddy. That is certainly a story worth telling—not just for a few weeks, but for generations.

> *Joshua set up the twelve stones that had been in the middle of the Jordan at the spot where the priests who carried the ark of the covenant had stood. And they are there to this day.* -Joshua 4:9, NIV

"And they are there to this day."
Think about that for a moment.
What stories are you telling? What spiritual legacy are you leaving for future generations?

● ● ●

Overall, this book has attempted to be like the oxygen mask on the airplane. What's the common rule we've all heard a thousand times? *Secure your own mask before attempting to help others.*

Hopefully, by this point, you have come to realize in your heart that your story matters and you have a story to tell. My prayer is that you are piecing together the story-building encounters you have already had with the Lord, or are pursuing this level of relationship. I get it; life is full of busyness and it can be easy to just go through the motions, but God desires us to weave our stories into the larger Story that He is writing.

Regardless of where you fall, this book is like the oxygen mask. Now that you've secured it—now that you have defined your story—it's time to help others.

Whether you realize it or not, you've got a story to tell, and by pointing to the moments of breakthrough you've had in your journey with God, you can help others create their own stories.

Simon Sinek, best-selling author of *Start with Why* and *Leaders Eat Last*, often speaks to the interesting dilemma that has been created over the past couple of decades by the explosion of the self-help industry. We see the prominent "self-help" section in our local bookstore, but what we really need is a "help others" section.

Something powerful happens when you realize that this is bigger than you—this life is about more than your personal comfort, safety, and security; it's about more than building your own personal empire or pursuing the American Dream without stopping to consider those in need right in front of you. There is a shift that is taking place in many circles—and not just Christian circles—as more and more people realize that "self-help" actually takes place when we pour ourselves out for the sake of others.

There's a story that Chris Hodges, pastor of Alabama's *Church of the Highlands*, once told about a woman who came to him because she was feeling like her life lacked purpose. On the surface, it seemed like she had everything she ever wanted; yet, something was missing. Chris suggested she get involved at the church's Dream Center, located near the heart of the city. This woman plugged in and began volunteering several hours a week—doing everything from baking cookies to having simple conversations with people less fortunate than herself.

Some time passed, and Chris ran into this woman at the church. She seemed like a completely different person; the joy on her face was evident. When he asked how she was doing and commented that she had not been in for counseling in awhile, the woman explained that she was so busy serving others that she had completely forgotten about her own problems.

Addressing his congregation, Pastor Chris said that he could give them advice all day long—even good, biblical advice—but he realized that what many of them actually needed was to get out and serve someone.

Perhaps there is a teenager in your church who doesn't have a father figure and needs some advice for the road ahead.

Perhaps there is a single mom you know that has her hands full and needs another woman to come alongside her as a mentor.

Perhaps there is a nearby college student who is far from home and would give anything for a hot meal and time around a table with a joy-filled family.

Regardless of what it looks like, I hope you can find the Dan Berlin in your life—someone that desires to do great things, but has a few limitations. Someone that has vision, yet finds themselves blind. Someone that needs a guiding hand in their journey. This doesn't have to be a physical handicap; almost everyone has something that is preventing them from getting to the next level. No matter what it is, they need you. They need you to share your story and help them create their own.

When you read the Story the Bible tells you'll see that we win in the end but there is still plenty of work to be done in the meantime. Let us come together and stand at the forefront of the "help others" industry. It all starts when you realize your story has value and begin to *tell it well.*

Not everyone is going to write a book about their lives and sell it on bookshelves. But we all write a story through our lives that will be read by those around us. And through that, we have an opportunity to have an impact by touching just one other person. And that, by extension, will change the world.
-Carlos Whittaker

ACKNOWLEDGEMENTS

My wonderful wife, Maritza - Thank you for letting me pour my heart and soul into this project, for all the late nights, and for putting up with my obsession with fulfilling this dream. You're the best and I love your hair by the way.

Isabella & Caleb - You can't read this yet, but you were in the forefront of my mind through this whole process. Books are great, but you two are my biggest spiritual legacy.

Mom & Dad - Thanks for bringing me in to the world 30 years ago and trusting the Lord with your children's lives. You've created an incredible family tree with deep roots, ready for the long haul. Your ceiling is my floor, and I don't take that for granted. Love you.

Jared Stump - You're proof that not all heroes wear capes—some wear white guy glasses. You're a true publishing expert; thanks for navigating this journey with me and taking the guesswork out of the process. You make me a better author, and watching your skills and career evolve over the past 7+ years of our friendship has been a joy.

Kyle Embry - Some of my favorite moments in ministry have happened when I was a part of your team. You're a great leader and an absolute nut—in a good way. Thank you for taking me under your wing and representing what a ministry of passion, integrity, and God-stories should look like.

Danny & Diane McDaniel - Your ability to gently prod someone toward their destiny is unparalleled. Thank you for encouraging me to never settle for normal by exemplifying a life filled with adventure and obedience.

To my siblings: Cara, Mark, Alex, Josh, and Nathan - I love that you're my family. We have some crazy stories! In fact, I wrote several in this book initially but cut them out because they just seemed too outrageous. Flaming Jeeps, anyone?

Daniel Hannon - Your friendship has been game-changing in my life. I can truly say that this book would not have made it to print if not for some of the projects we've launched together. Your drive for excellence, learning, and no-nonsense approach to life makes me want to be better.

Jeri Hill - Steve had the most incredible impact on my life and I can't even begin to describe how thankful I am for his life. Thank you for planting the church when you did, and for the school of ministry. It changed everything.

Daniel & Jenna Norris - You showed me what a true Spirit-filled youth ministry should look like, and that sealed my heart to never settle for less than the full Gospel. Thanks for stripping away the games and fluff and focusing on the presence of the One that matters.

Bob & Polly Hamp - Bob, this book was dead in the water until I attended your publishing workshop. Thank you for making publishing seem within reach and for resurrecting this project in my heart. Polly, your session at said workshop inspired me to switch up a few chapters and make the intro a little bit more engaging.

Mary & Steve Brailo - Thank you for mentoring and pouring into a young group of punks at a small church in Easton, PA. You live like Jesus and I am thankful for your time and influence in my young life.

Jon Acuff - Other than meeting briefly at an event you spoke at, you don't know me but you've been a huge inspiration to an aspiring author and businessman. Thanks for demonstrating the perfect combo of humor, hustle, and practical writing.

Robert Morris - We've also only briefly met, but your teachings have changed my life. Thank you for leading the Church well and demonstrating a high level of integrity and honesty.

To the *Tell It Well* **Launch Team** - Thank you for embracing the message of this project and committing to help share it with the world. You're incredible humans & your feedback along the journey has been crucial. (Gary, Sabrina, Ryan, Tiffanee, Jacob, Randy, Ricky, Ashlie, Chuck, Ana Marie, Brent, Brandon, Ryan, Cody, April, Cam, Stephani, Paul, Ben, Keegan, Jonathan, Meredith, Meghan, and Amanda)

Contact Luke

My heart behind this book is not to simply broadcast a message
(although that's part of it) but to begin a conversation. I'd love to
continue the conversation outside of these pages, and I'm very
accessible! I'll happily sit down for lunch, come speak at your event,
or just answer questions you have about storytelling, Christianity,
creativity, or anything in between.

me@lukegajary.com
facebook.com/lukegajary
instagram.com/lukegajary
twitter.com/lukegajary
lukegajary.com

ENDNOTES

Chapter 2
1 - Mark Batterson, *Chase the Lion* (Colorado Springs: Multnomah, 2016), 80.

Chapter 4
2 - Donald Miller, *A Million Miles in a Thousand Years: What I Learned While Editing My Life* (Nashville: Thomas Nelson, 2008), 59.

Chapter 7
3 - Text in italics is taken from the Global Anabaptist Mennonite Encyclopedia, Online Edition. Edits have been made for length and clarity.

Chapter 9
4 - My primary sources for this quote from Steve's journal and general information on the Brownsville Revival were taken from blog/news articles posted on www.voiceofrevolution.com and the Toledo Blade. These sources are quoted multiple times in this section.

5 - Jonathan Malm, *Unwelcome: 50 Ways Churches Drive Away First-Time Visitors* (Los Angeles: Center for Church Communication, 2014), 69-71.
Chapter 10
6 - Pastor Steve Hill, Raising Up World Changers (Chapel service at Heartland School of Ministry), February 11, 2007.

Chapter 12
7 - The Scriptures used here are taken from Ephesians 1:1, Philippians 1:1, Galatians 1:2, and 1 Corinthians 1:2.
8 - This is a paraphrase based on Dan's account of the situation to me.

Chapter 18
9 - runnersworld.com/general-interest/visually-impaired-athlete-runs-inca-trail-to-machu-picchu-in-one-day
10 - coloradoan.com/story/sports/2014/10/08/blind-fort-collins-man-first-ro-run-across-grand-canyon/16943327/ — Excerpts from Dan, Alison, and Charles used by permission.